NO
OTHER
gods
BEFORE
ME

NATHAN MARTIN

NO OTHER *gods* BEFORE ME

A CALL TO WORSHIP
THE ONE TRUE GOD

No Other gods Before ME
A Call To Worship The One True God

© 2025 by Nathan Martin

Published by Truth Book Company, LLC
Anderson, IN

ISBN 978-1-965584-20-0, *paperback*

Cover Design & Typesetting: Truth Book Company, LLC

We hope you enjoy this book from Truth Book Company. Our goal is to provide high-quality, Bible-based books, curriculum, and resources to equip you to stand for truth.

For more information on our other books and resources, special discounts, bulk purchases, or hosting a live event, please visit **www.truthbook.co.**

ACKNOWLEDGEMENTS

This book was brought to life by the help of many. My deepest gratitude is in order to countless individuals, including:

Sister Renae Chessor and the "Door of Hope" community at the Keystone Apostolic Church; Our series on idolatry provided the groundwork to write this book.

My wife, Tiffany, who always granted me a listening ear as I wrestled in the writing process.

Keenan and Felicia Hoffman for reading through my drafts and offering encouragement.

William "Bill" Peckol, who offered his meticulous editing expertise.

The Keystone Apostolic Church, because you're a haven for making disciples, much content was inspired by your example.

Pastor James Chessor for writing the Foreword.

LJ Harry for the timely phone calls and encouragement

Brother Nate Whitley for his thoughtful review and kind words gracing the back cover.

Jordon Frye, Steven Gill, and Truth Book Company for believing in this work and bringing it to publication.

Table of Contents

Foreword

I don't remember when I first met Bro. Nathan Martin. It had to be during a revival I preached in Charleston back in 2011. I can't recall the exact moment, but what I do know is that it feels like he's always been a part of my life. Some connections are just like that—God-ordained, not easily explained.

Since the summer of 2013, when my family and I moved to West Virginia, Bro. Martin and I have served side by side in ministry. For twelve years now, I've watched him live what he preaches. He's a man of faith, integrity, and conviction. He has stood with me through thick and thin, and I've watched God shape him into the servant leader he is today.

This book, No Other gods Before ME, is a powerful and timely word for this generation. It isn't just written truth, it's lived truth. Nathan hasn't just studied this subject—he's wrestled with it. He's wept over it. He's prayed his way through every page. This is not a side note in his life, but a message that's been carved out of deep devotion and personal consecration.

What you'll find in these pages is bold, biblical, and straightforward. It's a call back to the altar; a call to put God first again. It is a call to put God first, not in theory, not in lip service, but in the hidden places of our hearts and the decisions of our daily lives. Bro Martin deals with the subtle idols that sneak into our thinking, our habits, and even our churches. He doesn't do it with harshness, but with clarity. He sounds the alarm, and he points us to Jesus.

As his Pastor, I am proud of him—proud of this work and of the man behind it. This is his first book, but it reads like something born of years of prayer and faithfulness, because it is.

My encouragement to every reader: Don't treat this like another book. Treat it like a mirror. Let it confront, convict, and call you deeper. Read it slow. Pray while you read. Let God speak to you through it.

I thank God for Bro. Nathan Martin. I thank God for this message. I pray every person who opens this book feels the same call I feel—the call to worship God alone, with nothing else before Him.

—*Pastor James Chessor*
Keystone Apostolic Church

Preface

In the book of Exodus, God gave His people the foundation of all the commandments: "…Thou shalt have no other gods before me." Instead of crediting the One True God, we strive to crown ourselves as "god" by constructing idols that appeal to our fallen nature. Ironically, idolatry often masks self-worship, as we shape our gods in ways that ultimately reflect and serve ourselves.

No matter a person's past, pedigree, or current position, we all carry the identity of worshiper. This fact forces us to ask multiple questions; What is worship? What am I worshiping? Why does it matter what I worship and why should I care?

As we journey through this book, we will confront the tension of honestly examining who we truly are. This examination brings us to a pivotal choice: will we surrender our lives to the One we were created to worship, or will we serve ourselves through the idols offered by the world?

Chapter 1:
What is Worship?

"Stay here with the donkey," Abraham told the servants. "The boy and I will travel a little farther. We will worship there, and then we will come right back." — (Genesis 22:5 NLT)

"How could God? Why would He promise us a son, fulfill His promise, then ask me to take away the life of the son He gave me?"

Could these have been the unspoken thoughts of Abraham as he lay in bed, watching the moonlight shine through the coarse, goat-haired tent ceiling? Perhaps his mind and heart were consumed by the weight of God's command etched deeply into his soul: 'Abraham...Take your only son, Isaac, to the land of Moriah and offer him as a burnt offering.' It's unwise to presume too much, but it's safe to say that even Abraham, the father of faith and friend of God, had a sleepless night. While bearing this burden, he probably did his best not to wear the weight of it on his shoulders.

The sleepless night likely brought an early rising. After he awoke his boy and servants, Abraham had to put faith into footsteps. If we place ourselves in the sandals of Abraham, we find it difficult to imagine faith moving us instead of fear; nevertheless, Abraham ascended Mount Moriah, ready to follow through in obedience, believing God would provide an offering and had the power to resurrect his son (Genesis 22:8; Hebrews 11:19). Regardless of trepidation, he remembered the promise that from Isaac would come a great nation (Genesis 17:16).

As readers, we are logically tempted to ask the question: "How could God even ask such a thing?" But, as is the case in every situation, God in His sovereignty always has a purpose and plan. Abraham, a man who relied on God's promises rather than explanations, understood this.

Through grueling trial, the story of Abraham reveals to us what to do when there is a great test – respond with great faith. In doing so, we galvanize our obedience to the Word of God. Even with complete trust and obedience, one can only imagine the compounding emotions Abraham must have felt as he took his son up the mountain. Isaac had the wood on his shoulders, while Abraham carried the knife. As they arrived where the sacrifice would be made, Abraham built an altar, arranged the wood, laid Isaac on the wood, and picked up the knife to kill the sacrifice…his son of promise.

At that exact moment, the provision of God showed up – the angel of the Lord cried out, telling him not to harm the boy. Abraham heard the call, and immediately his gaze was directed to a ram caught by its horns in a thicket. This substitute would be the sacrifice that would take the stead of Isaac (Genesis 22:13). Undoubtedly, it was Abraham's obedience that made way for God's provision. As we'll discuss in later chapters, in order to be pleasing to God, our feelings and emotions must take a back seat to obedience. Our choice to obey, regardless of our feelings, charts the course of our lives to the plan, presence, and provision of God.

How Could God?

When we look at the story of Abraham, we find that it is not only a template for how to respond to a test, but an incredible foreshadowing of the ultimate sacrifice that would come through God manifesting Himself in the flesh as Jesus Christ. When sin entered the world through Adam's disobedience, the fallen nature with its curses were passed on from generation to generation, the most significant being the curse of death. Paul wrote that the payment of sin is death (Romans 6:23).

Sin, self-gratification at the expense of everyone, always comes at the highest price; it separates us from God and our human relationships. Sin is the greatest divider of all mankind because its selfish nature includes a temporary pleasure with a destination of destruction. Romans 3:23 puts us all under this burden when it says, "For all have sinned, and come short of the glory of God."

So, what is the remedy? If all have sinned, and the punishment for sin is death, where is our hope of salvation? How is it possible for me to be in right standing with God? How can there be a reconciliation of relationship when sin has severed relational ties? The writer of the book of Hebrews speaks directly to these questions when he says, "Without the shedding of blood, there is no remission of sins" (Hebrews 9:22). To satisfy the justice of a holy God, a life had been given, unveiling the immeasurable depths of His love.

The method of the imperfect animal sacrifice riddled throughout the Old and New Testaments pointed forward to the perfect sacrifice that would come through Jesus Christ.

> The sacrifices under that system were repeated again and again, year after year, but they were never able to provide perfect cleansing for those who came to worship. If they could have provided perfect cleansing, the sacrifices would have stopped, for the worshipers would have been purified once for all time, and their feelings of guilt would have disappeared. But instead, those sacrifices actually reminded them of their sins year after year. For it is not possible for the blood of bulls and goats to take away sins. (Hebrews 10:1-4 NLT)

Humanity needed a sacrifice that would make the payment for sin and wash away the sin, guilt, and shame that accompany a life without God. His sacrifice opened the way to live in relationship with God. It was the God of all creation who robed Himself in flesh as the man Jesus Christ, fully God and fully man (Colossians 2:9), and became the perfect sacrifice through His sinless life. John the Baptist proclaimed He was the Lamb of God who willingly took upon Himself the sins of the world on the cross (John 1:29). Unlike the imperfect animal sacrifices that were only temporary, Jesus died once and for all (Hebrews 7:27).

So, why would God ask Abraham to sacrifice his son? Within the story of Abraham and Isaac, the reader will find many important parallels that can shed light on the purpose behind the story's inclusion in the text.

- This story foreshadows Jesus Christ taking the place of humanity as the sacrifice for sin. Isaac represents humanity, spared through the substitution of the ram. Just as God provided a ram for Abraham, this moment points prophetically to the day God would provide Himself as the ultimate sacrifice.

- The ram that replaced Isaac had its horns caught in a thicket (Genesis 22:13) while the Lamb of God bore on His head a crown of thorns (Matthew 27:29).

- Abraham said God would provide the sacrifice (Genesis 22:8) and Jesus was the "Lamb of God who takes away the sins of the world" (John 1:29).

This example only begins to plumb the depths of Old Testament narratives that direct us to Christ. It also addresses the question: "How could God?" Notice, with context, the manner and attitude in which we now ask the question. Now knowing the deeper meaning of it all, we follow up this question with:

"How could God love a sinner like me?"

"How could God manifest himself in the flesh and suffer unimaginably for me?"

"How could He foreknow all the mistakes I would make and pain I would inflict on myself and others, yet still give me a chance?"

Knowing this, we owe Him our lives. Knowing the debt He paid for all humanity, we are indebted to Him. We are called to worship Him, not out of obligation, but out of gratitude and love, knowing that "while we were yet sinners, Christ died for us" (Romans 5:8, KJV).

Worship Defined in the Old Testament

The word "worship" appears for the first time in Scripture when God commanded Abraham to sacrifice Isaac. When Abraham used the verb "worship," it is "*šâḥâ*" in Hebrew, meaning the action of bowing down. In modern terminology, we can equate worship to surrendering every part of ourselves. God provided a clear command: "For thou shalt worship no other god: for the Lord, whose name is Jealous, is a jealous God" (Exodus 34:14, KJV). God is not jealous of us, but for us. The Creator, who manifested Himself in Jesus Christ, died so we could come to salvation and relationship.

> *In modern terminology, we can equate worship to surrendering every part of ourselves*

This word *šâḥâ* is used in several connotations throughout the Old Testament and therefore doesn't isolate itself solely to the "bowing down" to the one true God. As worshipers, human beings express their worship in many forms throughout the Bible—often directing it toward idols and false gods, which are contrary to the will of God. Both through Scripture and history, we learn that we will meet the same fate as the object of our worship. Therefore, if we are *bowing down* our lives to Christ, we will find life;

if we shift our worship to anything else, we will find death and destruction.

Worship Defined in the New Testament

The Apostle Paul gave practical instruction to the church in Rome about worship when he wrote,

> I beseech you therefore, brethren, by the mercies of God, that ye present your bodies a living sacrifice, holy, acceptable unto God, which is your reasonable service. And be not conformed to this world: but be ye transformed by the renewing of your mind, that ye may prove what is that good, and acceptable, and perfect, will of God. (Romans 12:1-2, KJV)

The word "service" here is also rendered as "worship."

Jesus presented himself as the ultimate sacrifice through death, and it is our reasonable *worship* to present ourselves as a "living sacrifice."

Truths about Worship…Regardless of What You Worship

1. Worship is radical, never casual. It encompasses our lives and is not contained or compartmentalized. There is no such thing as a "part-time" worshiper.

2. Worship equates to sacrifice – it comes at a cost. We are always laying our lives down in the service of

something, and we subordinate ourselves to the object of our worship to receive the benefits or consequences of what we serve. When we gain the world, we lose our soul. When we gain Christ, we find life. Jesus instructed His disciples, "If any man will come after me, let him deny himself, and take up his cross, and follow me. For whosoever will save his life shall lose it: and whosoever will lose his life for my sake shall find it" (Matthew 16:24-25, KJV).

3. Worship is not just an action; it is the motive of the heart that works its way into our behaviors. What we do is not separate from who we are.

Christ's sacrifice on the cross is not automatically applied to our lives. He died, was buried, and rose on the third day so we can have the opportunity to identify with His death, burial, and resurrection through repentance, baptism in Jesus' name, and receiving the gift of the Holy Ghost (Romans 6:3-4; 8:9-11). In a world where the options to serve all things "anti-God" are endless, we can choose to serve the One whom we were created to worship.

Study Questions

1. What are some practical examples of 'dying-to-self' through the action of repentance?

2. What are ways that we can "present our bodies as a living sacrifice" that is holy, acceptable, and our reasonable worship according to Romans 12:1?

3. As you progress through the pages of this book, you'll identify what you've given your worship to. At this stage in the book, can you identify the areas in your life in which you are, perhaps, worshiping something other than God?

Chapter 2:
Idol Worship

> What people revere, they resemble, either for ruin or for restoration. – G.K. Beale

In the eyes of our modern culture, it is normal to idolize someone or something to the point of pursuing their likeness in hopes of finding fulfillment. Nevertheless, by doing so, we can easily underestimate the power of giving ourselves to serve anything other than Jesus. To give our time, energy, and essentially our lives in pursuit of anything other than Christ is not only destructive but leaves us unsatisfied.

The word "idol" recalls to mind images of wood and stone that ancient cultures crafted and worshiped as their gods. This practice remains present, not only in the third world, but in the United States. Most reading this book may not have a statue of Buddha on their bedside table or formally practice false religion, but we may possess idols in our life that we serve as our god.

Practically speaking, what is idol worship? Simply put, idol worship or idolatry is the worship of creation over creator. Along this definition, the list of examples to be offered is extensive, but let's start with the subject of money and possessions. It was Billy Graham who said, "Take,

Idol worship or idolatry is the worship of creation over creator.

for example, our preoccupation with money and material possessions. These aren't necessarily wrong, of course; we need them to take care of our loved ones and make our lives comfortable. But both can easily become "idols" that we slavishly follow and allow to become the most important things in our lives."[1]

According to Scripture, it is the *love* of money that is the root of all evil, not the money itself (1 Timothy 6:10). Jesus spoke in Matthew 6:24 that we cannot serve both God and Mammon (money). This doesn't mean we live as paupers barely scraping by; rather, we are to be committed to God and "Honor him with all of our substance" (Proverbs 3:9, KJV).

Money and possessions are not inherently wrong, but when they are prioritized before God, and our hearts are bent toward them, we have created an idol by worshiping creation over creator. This principle can be applied to relationships, careers, entertainment, and pleasures. All these things are necessary components of life. However, how one prioritizes them determines if it is an idol we are serving.

Let's look at the instructions of Jesus when He listed one of the requirements for becoming His disciple: "If any man come to me, and hate not his father, and mother, and wife, and children, and brethren, and sisters, yea, and his own life also, he cannot be my disciple" (Luke 14:26, KJV). No doubt, the word "hate" is strong and catches the reader's attention. One might ask themselves the question, "Is Jesus really telling me to hate my loved ones and my own life?" Contextually, the word "hate" is a term used in comparison. It is only in a comparative sense, as opposed to the literal, that the term can possibly be used.[2] Warren Wiersbe said, "We should love Christ so much that our love for family would be like hatred in comparison."

When we love Jesus first, we love others best. When we love God first, we set up a domino effect of honoring and loving others in the way God intended. As Paul wrote to the church in Rome, "The love of God is shed abroad in our hearts by the Holy Ghost" (Romans 5:5, KJV). When a husband is filled with the Spirit and walks in the Spirit, he loves his wife and children best. When an employee loves God first, she works her job for the glory of God, is faithful to the church, and is a giver to the kingdom of God. When we live in relationship with God, we find entertainment and pleasure in living for Him and choose to deny the path of sinful pleasures that destroy us and others. Inevitably, when we push God to the backseat of our lives, these vital elements meant to glorify and represent God become manipulated and deformed into sinful behaviors that take us away from the original plan of God.

If God is good and determines what is good, it is safe to say that the greatest evil is the perversion of the greatest good. For us to deconstruct and deform what He calls "good" to make it "better" is an act of pride and arrogance. Taking His design of marriage, relationships, purpose, and altering it to fit our desires is idolatry. Paul wrote to the church in Colossae, "So put to death the sinful, earthly things lurking within you. Have nothing to do with sexual immorality, impurity, lust, and evil desires. Don't be greedy, for a greedy person is an idolater, worshiping the things of this world" (Colossians 3:5, NLT).

> *The greatest evil is the perversion of the greatest good.*

Next, let us dive into humanity's first instance of idolatry. It just so happens that we find the genesis…in Genesis.

Idolatry in Genesis

From our first breath, we have the choice of who and what we will serve. Free will is a gift from our Creator. The ability to choose was no different for Adam and Eve. As the first man and woman created in the image of God, they bore the image of God along with many of His characteristics. In the Garden of Eden, they had a daily relationship with God and each other, feeling no pain, suffering, or death. Their purpose was to be the viceroy of the earth and to have dominion over plant life and living creatures. Just imagine, they were in such perfect union with God that they communed with Him face to face. Eden was not just paradise in name only.

Nevertheless, paradise came to a tragic end in Genesis chapter three when Adam ate of the fruit of the "tree of knowledge of good and evil," breaking the commandment given from God that they ought to abstain from that tree. Scripture says that Eve was deceived, but Adam disobeyed with open eyes; he was responsible for what happened that day in the Garden of Eden.

So, where is idolatry in this story? Through the deceptive conversation with the serpent that caused Eve to question God, she followed through with the temptation presented to her. Rather than seeing all her heavenly Father had given her and Adam, she missed the "forest for the tree." She succumbed to the desire for the one thing she could not have. The fall of humanity started here:

> And when the woman saw that the tree was good for food, and that it was pleasant to the eyes, and a tree to be desired to make one wise, she took of the fruit thereof, and did eat,

and gave also unto her husband with her; and he did eat. (Genesis 3:6, KJV)

Once Eve ate, her husband, who stood idly by, ate as well. It was his disobedience that caused sin and death to enter the world (Romans 5:12). The reader finds the immediate effects of sin even before God named the consequences of their actions (see Genesis 3:14-19):

- They were afraid and hid themselves from God.

- They were ashamed to discover their nakedness and attempted to cover themselves. Their relationship with God and each other was severed by the unloving act of sin.

- After hiding from God and finally answering His question, 'Did you do the one thing I told you not to do?' they refused to take accountability. Adam said, 'The women YOU gave me made me do this!' Eve said, 'It was the SERPANT that tricked me!'

Notice how prior to their fall, Adam and Eve bore the image of God and His characteristics. After the fall, their identity shifted. Disobedience caused a degeneration. Rather than projecting the image of God, they took on the features of the serpent: craftiness, manipulation, deception, and blame-shifting.

From the story of Adam and Eve, the question begs: "In the moment they sinned, who were they worshiping?" Adam and Eve, who bore the image of God and walked in perfect relationship with their creator, through disobedience, took on the characteristics of the serpent. However, in disobedience, the object of Adam and Eve's worship became themselves. In many ways, idol worship is simply the conduit to the worship of self. When worshiping creation over Creator, we practice the sin of pride. Think about it. All forms of idolatry, whether seeking material gain, notoriety, addiction, or relationships, *Idol worship is simply the conduit to the worship of self.* is a direct conduit to the worship of: (insert your name). Herein is found the deluded reasoning we often practice, placing creation over Creator. It all goes back to the desire of self. The propensity to replace the one true God with an inadequate substitute leaves us dissatisfied and broken as we succumb to the same temptations of the lust of the flesh, the lust of the eyes, and the pride of life (1 John 2:16).

Since Genesis 3:6, humanity has shown its proclivity to seek independence outside of God. The hard reality is that our human nature cries out to be a god through selfish behavior like trusting in ourselves, feelings, desires, and striving to dictate our destiny. This leads us to break the commands of a loving God and sin by seeking self-gratification at the expense of another. Thinking we know what's best leads us to walk repeatedly into the same trap of failure and destruction, believing we'll obtain a preferred result. In this way, we live out "achieving" the definition of insanity: seeking new results from the same practices.

Our opening quote, "What people revere, they resemble, either for ruin or for restoration," speaks volumes. When we worship anything other than God, we resemble it and fall into ruin. Adam's choice to sin cascaded the world into ruin. The fabric of fellowship was ripped apart by his choice. As Paul wrote in Romans, "When Adam sinned, sin entered the world. Adam's sin brought death, so death spread to everyone, for everyone sinned" (Romans 5:12, NLT). But thanks be to God that Jesus Christ, the second Adam (1 Cor. 15:45-47), is the reverse of the curse:

> Yes, Adam's one sin brings condemnation for everyone, but Christ's one act of righteousness brings a right relationship with God and new life for everyone. Because one person disobeyed God, many became sinners. But because one other person obeyed God, many will be made righteous. (Romans 5:18-19, NLT)

Jesus, God in the flesh, represented everything Adam was meant to be. He perfectly bore the image of God, walked in dominion/authority, and was tempted as we are, yet He never sinned. He took on the sins of the world through His death, burial, and resurrection. When we surrender our lives to Jesus, our lives reverse from ruin to restoration, and we no longer are bound by sin and condemnation.

Study Questions

1. If we resemble what we worship, how does idolatry reveal itself in our private and public life? Can idol worship in any form be "contained" and never reveal itself?

2. Pride and shame are different sides of the same coin… both the extremes of self. The antidote to combat them is humility. What is the scriptural definition of humility and how do we put it into practice?

Chapter 3:
The Worship of ME

> *And remember, when you are being tempted, do not say, "God is tempting me." God is never tempted to do wrong, and he never tempts anyone else. Temptation comes from our own desires, which entice us and drag us away. These desires give birth to sinful actions. And when sin is allowed to grow, it gives birth to death. — (James 1:13-15, NLT)*

The typewriter, telegraph, and light bulb were invented during the Industrial Revolution, but the watershed moment that altered history forever was the creation of the steam engine. Coined as the invention that turned the wheels of mechanized factory production, this machine catalyzed the Industrial Revolution by powering ships, trains, and eventually cars. [3]

As Manifest Destiny became more ambitious in the 1800s, the steam locomotive was a fixture in accomplishing western expansion by connecting the coasts by railroad. The need for efficient transportation that superseded horse and buggy made its way into legislation on

July 1, 1862, when President Lincoln authorized the Pacific Railway Act to begin the construction of the First Transcontinental Railroad.

Many great feats were accomplished with one railroad company starting in Sacramento, California, and another in Omaha, Nebraska, striving to meet in the middle. Those embarking from Sacramento had to contend with the rugged terrain of the Sierra Nevada Mountains, while blasting tunnels and laying track through solid granite. Those starting in Omaha confronted the Great Plains, the Rocky Mountains, and the harsh Wyoming winters.[4] Without the invention of the steam engine propelling our country to the new age of technology and growth, who knows what our country and world would look like today?

"Desire" can be compared to the steam engine that makes the train go. As one writer aptly described, "Turn off the steam, and you have no power. Let the steam go its own way, and you have destruction."[5] Desire, a necessary factor that motivates us, if channeled outside of the will of God, is a recipe for disaster.

Desire, a necessary factor that motivates us, if channeled outside of the will of God is a recipe for disaster.

To continue this same "train" of thought, desire in its fundamental form was given to you by God. Desires embedded in our identity drive us. However, we must hitch our lives to God's design for these desires rather than letting the steam go its own way, our lives derailing with destructive cargo.

Paul urged the church to unhitch from what lurks within us and have nothing to do with "sexual immorality, impurity, lust, and evil desires" (Colossians 3:5, NLT). He went on to list more proverbial "railcars" we must detach from:

> But now is the time to get rid of anger, rage, malicious behavior, slander, and dirty language. Don't lie to each other, for you have stripped off your old sinful nature and all its wicked deeds. (Colossians 3:8-9, NLT)

He relayed the same words to the church in Ephesus and adds that they "instead, be kind to each other, tenderhearted, forgiving one another, just as God through Christ has forgiven you" (Ephesians 4:32, NLT). In context, these letters from Paul are to the church; those who have already been born again of the water and the Spirit. The unconverted are not addressed here because they have not detached from the world and turned to God through repentance.

Paul admonished the churches that the old fallen nature and the desires that accompany it are to be "put off." A living man doesn't wear dead men's clothes. Likewise, we cannot be a new creation (by being born-again) yet practice the old lifestyle and rebellion that we put off.

Many are deceived into thinking they can simultaneously follow Jesus and whatever path of desire they want. This self-deception is often justified on the basis that they have "confessed their faith in Christ" and believe there is no need for change. Paul dispels the idea that the old nature (with its desires) and the new nature can coincide when he declares:

> Since you have heard about Jesus and have learned the truth that comes from him, throw off your old sinful nature and your former way of life, which is corrupted by lust and deception. Instead, let the Spirit renew your thoughts and attitudes. Put on your new nature, created to be like God— truly righteous and holy. (Ephesians 4:21-24, NLT)

Has God Set Me Up?

Eve saw that the fruit of the tree of the knowledge of good and evil was "desired to make one wise." James reminds us that even though God placed desire within our identity, He never tempts us to sin. God has not set you up to fail; rather, we have been granted the gift of choice. It is not a sin to be tempted, but it is a sin to succumb to the temptation. It was Jesus who was tempted yet never sinned (Hebrews 4:15). Ultimately, we choose what we serve and what we give our desires over to.

Not unlike Genesis, the book of James reminds us what happens when we give in to selfish and sinful desires.

James compared temptation to an angler baiting a hook to catch a fish (James 1:13-15).

Sin culminates through the "Look, Lust, and Lure." For James' analogy, the bait is TEMPTATION and the hook that hides within is SIN.

1. The Look – The bait is cast in our line of vision.

2. The Lust – Our fleshly desires become fixated on the bait because it appeals to the appetite. Because of the fixation on the bait, the hook is not seen, or it is ignored.

3. The Lure – Our "own desires" entice us to chase the bait, not the hook. *If* we take the bait, the hidden hook comes with it.

Just as a fish will not willingly latch onto a naked hook, no sane person would willingly choose the consequences of sin without its bait. It is not the hook that draws us, but it's the bait. The allure of sin appears promising, but like the old maxim, "Sin will take you farther than you want to go, keep you longer than you want to stay, and cost you more than you want to pay." The pleasure of sin lasts for a season (Hebrews 11:25), and for the fish, it is only a moment before it becomes a fish out of water. Some think they can nibble at temptation and not get the hook. The drive to fulfill the carnal appetite leads to self-deception to believe that all is well until there is a reckoning. "For the wages of sin is death; but the gift of God is eternal life through Jesus Christ our Lord" (Romans 6:23, KJV). When the payment comes due, we are surprised by the pain and sorrow that is inflicted. I once heard it said like this: "Sin wouldn't be so attractive if the wages were paid immediately."

In James, the imagery changes from fishing to birthing (James 1:15). Sinful desires give birth to sinful actions. When allowed to grow, sin brings forth death. In this depraved state, we cannot save ourselves. It's only by turning away from sin and unto God in the form of repentance that we can begin the journey of salvation. "For the kind of sorrow God wants us to experience leads us away from sin and results in salvation. There's no regret for that kind of sorrow. But worldly sorrow, which lacks repentance, results in spiritual death" (2 Corinthians 7:10, NLT). Repentance doesn't mean that we are let off the hook for our actions, only to repeatedly chase the same temptation again. Persuading ourselves that we can live in a catch-and-release pond of salvation is a cycle of chaos. Perpetually getting snagged, crying out for God's help and forgiveness, then happily returning to the trap abuses the grace of God. Those who repeatedly sin, regardless of the consequences, have fallen into a place of self-deception and bondage. Freedom only begins when we shift our voracious craving for the bait to a voracious craving for repentance. Paul's words are potent when he describes those who refuse to repent as "enemies

THE WORSHIP OF ME

of the cross." Boldly, he declares how their god is their belly because they mind only earthly things that serve their appetites (Philippians 3:18-19).

How About I Just Get Rid of Desire?

We must ask ourselves how to navigate through temptation. Let's ponder a radical question: "If desire is what gets me in trouble, then shouldn't I try to destroy every desire I have?" Perhaps we should never want anything. Perhaps we ought to live as a robot that never feels or enjoys any form of life due to the fear of taking the bait to a desire that is sinful and destructive. Perhaps locking ourselves up in a monastery and secluding ourselves from society is the answer. Of course, many will understand that this response to temptation is not a reasonable one at all.

Again, desire in its basic form was given to us by our Creator. If you never felt hunger or thirst, you would never desire to eat or drink. If you never felt tired, you would never rest and therefore would wear away. Sex is a normal desire; without it, the human race could not continue. But when one pursues satisfying these desires in ways outside of God's will, trouble comes. Eating is normal; gluttony is sin. Sleep is normal; laziness is sin. "Marriage is honorable in all, and the bed undefiled; but whoremongers and adulterers God will judge" (Hebrews 13:4, KJV).[vi]

In the Old Testament, desire is attributed to appetite. In other words, it is something like longing to partake of something that will sustain and satisfy our inner longings. We are always seeking to eat – always seeking fulfillment. As humans, we're always looking for satisfaction physically, emotionally, mentally, and spiritually. Desire is so fundamental to our existence that we can look to the Bible for examples of how harmful it can be when desire is lost.

When someone has lost their appetite, it's attributed to something being wrong. In Job, Elihu asserted the timeless truth that when one is sick and hopeless, "they lose their appetite for even the most delicious food" (Job 33:20, NLT). When a man is sick and in despair, he loses his appetite. There are moments in life when we can sink into such a place of despair that all our wants, dreams, and aspirations are lost. Whether it is by unwarranted suffering that accompanies life or by the consequences of our own poor decisions, desires can dissipate through circumstances. However, in holding on at the point of despair, desire will restore itself, and you will seek to eat again. At that point, when desire returns, we must decide how we will satisfy our inner longings.

I Can't Get No Satisfaction

In 1965, the Rolling Stones' song, "Satisfaction," hit the airways with its famous double-negative line, "I can't get no satisfaction." This secular song is a mantra that speaks to every generation's endless pursuit for more. Solomon was ahead of this when he wrote, "The eyes of man are never satisfied" (Proverbs 27:20). Carnal desires are never satisfied in our incessant need for more. Our fallen nature has an insatiable stomach and, when fed, only provides temporary satisfaction, not permanent fulfillment. Raymond Woodward accurately detailed examples of this sort of appetite:

An appetite by its very nature can never be fully and finally satisfied, it can only be temporarily quenched. Human beings have many "unquenchable thirsts" – stuff, money, recognition, success, progress, happiness, intimacy, sex, relationship, partnership, friendship, fun, accomplishment … we never get "enough" of these things! [6]

It's common self-deception for those battling any particular sin, especially addiction, to deceive themselves into believing that they can indulge their sin one more time in order to satiate their desire. C.S. Lewis said, "Appetites grow through indulgence – not neglect. Gluttons think just as much about food as starving people." In other words, the more you feed an appetite, the more it escalates in intensity.[6] In other words, it's a bad idea to think to yourself, "How do I know what's good unless I try the bad?" The philosophy of experimenting with everything so you can later choose what's right because you've experienced what's wrong is foolish. Scripture calls us to "Taste and see that the Lord is good (Psalm 34:8),"while simultaneously the world promotes the same message about itself. No matter which path we choose, the concept of tasting and seeing is found. When Adam and Eve tasted disobedience, their eyes were opened. As it was with them, so it is with us; Our eyes are often bigger than our stomachs, believing we can digest our poor choices until we see the overwhelming guilt and shame that cannot be resolved. Rather than seeking to modify our desires, our goal should be transformation. To taste the goodness of God through His Word and Spirit opens our eyes to our lost condition and provides a path for us to surrender our desires to Him.

Transformed Desires

If we don't channel our desires toward our Creator, we will go through an endless cycle of chasing promising substitutes, often ignoring the hook that is lying in wait. Worldly pleasures cannot satisfy our hungry souls. No ungodly relationship, drug, or any form of sinful gratification can satisfy the hunger we have. It's only through salvation and relationship with Jesus that we can be fulfilled.

The worship of *me* begins with pursuing my selfish desires, exalting my broken image rather than the image of God. Therefore, there must be a transformation of my desires that can only come from repentance, baptism in the name of Jesus, and being filled with the gift of the

Holy Ghost. Several forms of transformation accompany the infilling of the Spirit of God: (1) Sin is unloving, but the "love of God is shed abroad in our hearts by the Holy Ghost" (Romans 5:5, KJV). (2) Living in sin is

> *The worship of me begins with pursuing my selfish desires.*

living in bondage, but being filled with the Spirit is freedom (2 Corinthians 3:17). (3) Sin deforms us; it removes the image of God. However, we are changed into His image by the Spirit (2 Corinthians 3:18). Paul wrote in Colossians that we ought to "put off the old man and his deeds," and "put on the new man" that reflects the image of the Creator (Colossians 3:9-10). This is accomplished by being filled with the Spirit.

As we close this chapter, remember that it is of the utmost importance to be filled with the Holy Ghost and to be led by the Spirit of God.

Feed Your Transformed Desires

But I say, walk by the Spirit, and you will not gratify the desires of the flesh. For the desires of the flesh are against the Spirit, and the desires of the Spirit are against the flesh, for these are opposed to each other, to keep you from doing the things you want to do. — (Galatians 5:16-17, ESV)

This is the call of the born-again believer: Starve the cravings of the flesh and walk in the Spirit. If we live in a daily relationship with God, we will not gratify our flesh. However, our 'old self' and its desires do not evaporate at our conversion, never to be seen again.[7] Even though we are crucified with Christ and are no longer enslaved to sin, we still choose to either feed the things of God or our flesh. Simply put, whatever we feed grows. We also discover our taste buds change with our new diet. Where we used to digest the garbage of the world, now we're partaking of the Bread of Life.

Tips to Feeding Your Transformed Desires:

1. **Daily connect with Jesus through prayer** – Do not treat God as the one to go to only when you are in need of something, or when you need 'out' of something. Living a prayerless life is the primary evidence of pride because it is as if we are saying, "I've got this!" Prayer should be the centerpiece of our lives. All must cultivate a relationship with our Father through sincere prayer.

2. **Feast on the Word of God** - Many ask God to speak into their lives. At the same time, many fail to search out His written Word to hear His voice. How can we continue a path of transformation when we're not digesting the scriptures? Obedience, maturation, and the ability to share the Gospel are impossible without knowing God through the scriptures. Those who refuse to study the "Word that's a lamp unto my feet

and a light unto my path" (Psalm 119:105 KJV) are guaranteed to walk their own path, often convincing themselves that they are in the will of God.

3. **Have a strategy for temptation** - Learning to combat the bait cast in our line of sight is very important. However, there are some ponds we shouldn't be in to begin with. Upon conversion, it may be necessary to cut close ties of fellowship with those who engage in ungodliness and influence us negatively. By simply changing our environment, we will remove a large portion of temptation. For those who have a history of addiction, removing yourself from the proximity of the temptation will do wonders. This principle applies to all believers because we are called to be separated from the world and unto Christ. Being faithful to God and the Body of Christ is our recipe for success.

4. **Know you'll still have temptations** – Even when we have a daily strategy to oppose ungodliness and participate in feeding the "new man," we will still be presented with temptations. Paul gives us hope in that "God is faithful, who will not suffer you to be tempted above that ye are able; but will with the temptation also make a way to escape, that ye may be able to bear it" (1 Corinthians 10:13, KJV). The "way of escape" is like a mountain pass that may not be an easy path. The rugged terrain of accountability and discomfort is not forced upon us, but it is the path that leads away from destruction and into life.

5. **Delight in the Lord** - "Blessed are those who hunger and thirst for righteousness, for they shall be filled" (Matthew 5:6). God does not give us the desires of a carnal, fallen, hardened heart. Instead, our new hearts crave God. It's through our daily walk with God that we realize satisfaction and fulfillment come from Him. When we are born again, our desire is for righteousness, and God satisfies that desire by giving us what we want – more of Him. No longer is our god our belly (gorging on our own desires as described in Philippians 3). Instead, out of our belly flows rivers of living water that quench our thirst.

Therefore, we can cling to the words of the Psalmist David:

Delight yourself in the Lord, and he will give you the desires of your heart. (Psalm 37:4, ESV)

Study Questions

1. Psalms 34:8 says, "Taste and see that the Lord is good." Taste means to feed upon, not to nibble or sip. What are practical daily disciplines you can institute in your life to nourish your walk with God?

2. 1 Corinthians 10:13 says, "There hath no temptation taken you but such as is common to man: but God is faithful, who will not suffer you to be tempted above that ye are able; but will with the temptation also make a way to escape, that ye may be able to bear it." Paul followed this verse up by saying to "flee from idolatry." God will provide us the option to escape temptation, but we must also run from idolatry. Rather than fighting, what are some idols in your life that you need to run away from?

Chapter 4:
We Become
What We Worship

People will always reflect something, whether it be God's character or some feature of the world. If people are committed to God, they will become like him; if they are committed to something other than God, they will become like that thing, always spiritually inanimate and empty like the lifeless and vain aspect of creation to which they have committed themselves. – G.K. Beale

Much of my book was inspired by *We Become What We Worship: A Biblical Theology of Idolatry*. You might notice that the title of Beale's work was not *We Become Like What We Worship*. Beale explains:

The thesis of the book is not that people become the idols they worship or become the God they worship, but they become *like* the idols or *like* God. The point of figuratively omitting the word *like* is to emphasize that the worshiper reflects some of the important qualities or attributes of the object of worship.[8]

Using Beale's approach, we can infer that whatever we worship determines our identity, fate, and legacy. When we are filled with the Spirit of God, we reflect His likeness. But what about when we are harboring idols? Throughout the Old Testament, the nation of Israel provides a case study in answering this question.

Place yourself in the position of an Israelite. Imagine the astounding works of God you've witnessed. Your God has just defeated the "gods" of Egypt with the plagues. You've watched Him wield the wind to make two invisible dams splitting the Red Sea open so you can walk on dry ground. Although the army of Pharaoh with its horses and chariots followed you out of your slavery, God promised you that "The Egyptians you see today, you will see no more (Exodus 14:13 KJV)." God released the waters upon the Egyptians, destroying all the enemies that tried to pursue you. Nevertheless, while you and the other Israelites praised God for His miracles, you are quick to forget His commandments and ask Aaron to make you a golden calf to worship instead. Aaron crafts the idol and responds: "These are your gods, Israel, who brought you out of Egypt" (Exodus 32.4).

Genesis All Over Again

While Moses was communing with God and receiving the Ten Commandments, Israel broke the first two: 1. Have no other gods before me. 2. Make no graven images.

Like impatient children, the people pressured Aaron to "make us gods who will go before us." Aaron complies with the people. He took their gold, melted it in the fire, and crafted the golden calf. The creation of the calf is not by accident. The behavior of the Israelites in the presence of the image that Aaron created was, perhaps, inspired by Apis, the Egyptian bull god often associated with fertility. After Moses descended the mountain with the tables of commandment in his hand, he sees the sheep are now like cattle running wild. Moses found the people in much the same state as the idolatrous nations of the world; they were eating, drinking, partying, and indulging in sexual immorality.

In many ways, the Israelites became like their treasured idol; the Lord told Moses that the Israelites were stiff-necked like an ox that doesn't respond when the reins are tugged. Like an ignorant bull, the Israelites were driven by stubbornness that resisted the love, provision, and fear of God. This story from Exodus is not unlike the third chapter of Genesis. In many ways, on a mass scale, it is what Paul referred to as "exchanging the glory of the immortal God for an image in the form of corruptible man and of birds and four-footed animals and crawling creatures" (Romans 1:23 NASB). Psalm 106 says, "They traded their glorious God for a statue of a grass-eating bull" (Psalms 106:20, NLT). Israel traded the image of God for a carved image that catered to their desires, making them less like God and more like beasts.

As appalling as it is, we have the same tendency following a great "exodus" of deliverance to reject our Savior. Instead of having hearts full of gratitude and indebtedness, often we stray from the shepherd, becoming like unrestrained cattle. We are warned in Proverbs about what can happen to us in this state: "Where there is no vision, the people are unrestrained, but happy is one who keeps the Law" (Proverbs 29:18 NASB). Impatience and a lack of trust in God often leads us to a "way that seems right to a man, but its end is the way of death" (Proverbs 14:12). Just as Israel chose to serve something that gave them permission to gratify their sinful appetites, we can create many excuses to divert our service away from the Creator to the poor substitute that is creation. The result? We wander aimlessly, letting our desires run wild.

Why Bow Down to a Golden Calf?

It took Israel one day to get out of Egypt, and 40 years to get Egypt out of Israel.

The longer you permit the culture of sin and bondage in your life, the more difficult it becomes to walk with God and be truly converted. Our new nature is not second nature – it must be cultivated. While it is true that we are as babes in Christ when we're born-again, sanctification and maturity occur through the work of the Spirit. Success in our walk with God is dependent upon certain disciplines like our trust in Jesus, faithfulness to prayer, commitment to the Word of

Our new nature is not second nature.

God and the church, and our daily habits to honor the God we are now "imaging." We, like Israel, can get out of Egypt, but still have Egypt in us if we're not filled with the Spirit of God and passionately pursuing our God. With Egypt still embedded in us, we'll follow Israel's example in Exodus 32. In the following section, let's compare Israel's thought process and our own.

First, when we're not vigilant in our trust and obedience to God, we often default to the familiarity of idols. Our vulnerability is found in trusting in what we feel rather than what we know. Times of uncertainty can drive us to be led by our emotions, gravitating to what's comfortable. When our feelings are in the driver's seat, our flesh will govern our decisions. We become a vehicle without brakes, bound to crash. When you're leaning on your emotions/ feelings, it is easy to trust a tangible god you can 'control.' For example, a zealous new convert (or any disciple for that matter) who doesn't continue in humility, teachability, and faithfulness to God and the church will not grow spiritually. Remaining spiritually immature leads to impatience, emotionalism, and a heart primed to become hardened by offense, justified or otherwise. Impulsivity characterizes those who are spiritually immature. Israel, instead of remembering the works of God, found it easier to give an ultimatum to their weak, stand-in leader to pacify their impatience. Attempting to strong-arm leadership, as Israel did to Aaron, reveals a spiritually immature posture, one driven by impatience, fear, and the desire for control. When leaders respond in an "Aaron-like" manner, yielding to pressure rather than guiding with conviction, the result is a distortion of true worship.

Many deceive themselves and attempt to deceive others by framing their desires as the "will of God." Many fall into this form of self-deception because they're tired of waiting obediently. The golden calf may have been inspired by Egypt, but Aaron attempted to portray the image as the God of Israel when he said, "Tomorrow is a feast to the Lord" (Exodus 32:5). In many ways, Aaron merged pagan practices with the worship of the God they were just beginning to become re-acquainted with.[9] To them, their compromise was the best of both worlds! To God, it was blatant sin and disregard for His unfailing love! Mixing ideology, culture, and extra-biblical traditions with the truth of God's Word is a god made in our own image. Paul told the Romans:

> Yes, they knew God, but they wouldn't worship him as God or even give him thanks. And they began to think up foolish ideas of what God was like. As a result, their minds became dark and confused. Claiming to be wise, they instead became

utter fools. And instead of worshiping the glorious, ever-living God, they worshiped idols made to look like mere people and birds and animals and reptiles. (Romans 1:21-23, NLT)

Simply put, humans can't resist the temptation to create God in their own image. Sometimes, the idols we fashion are made in an image beneath us.[10] When we refuse to worship Jesus as He truly is, we often come up with our own ideas about God. Nevertheless, while an idea about God may appear convincing on the surface, that does not mean it is necessarily an accurate depiction of who God is. Israel looked at a golden calf and said, "This is the god who brought us out of Egypt." What may seem absurd at first is in fact a common reality: people across the world, particularly in moments of desperation, often turn to gods of their own making.

"Sacred Cows"

When the truth of God's Word confronts your life, how do you respond? Do you conform to the Word, or do you merge bits of truth with your sense of justice, empathy, and need for happiness? Instead of looking to the Jesus who is the Way, the Truth, and the Life, do you manufacture your own "Jesus" that fits into your paradigm? There are countless ideologies about God that are false, but let's look at two common examples of this sort of merging that, in many ways, have become sacred cows of Christianity.

Prosperity Gospel

The so-called *Prosperity Gospel* is a teaching that equates God's favor with earthly wealth, health, and success. Its proponents often cite passages such as "Whatsoever he does shall prosper" (Psalm 1:3), "...that ye may prosper in all that you do" (Deuteronomy 29:9), or "...the wealth of the sinner is laid up for the just" (Proverbs 13:22), but rarely do they pause to examine these verses in their full biblical context. When read carefully, these passages speak of spiritual prosperity in the way of righteousness, not a divine guarantee of financial gain or trouble-free living.

At its core, this movement subtly reframes faith into a transactional tool, something to be "used" to unlock God's blessings rather than a humble trust in His character and will. Some of its most visible advocates are what some call *celebrity pastors*: leaders whose public image, branding, and personal wealth have become almost as prominent as their message. The Bible warns against this kind of self-promotion and the pursuit of spiritual influence for personal gain. In Acts 8, Simon the Sorcerer sought to purchase the power of the Holy Spirit so that he could use it to elevate himself. Peter rebuked him sharply, telling him, "Your heart is not right before God" (Acts 8:21). In a similar way, when pastors market the gospel as a means to increase their fame or fortune, they imitate Simon's error by seeking God's gifts as a pathway to personal glory rather than

God's glory. While influence, success, and even wealth is not inherently sinful, the underlying driver of the prosperity message often leans toward covetousness and turns the heart from God Himself to what He can give.

Paul warned Ephesus about those who "are greedy for more" (Ephesians 5:5), reminding believers that such desires can become a form of idolatry. He also tells the Colossians that covetousness is a form of idolatry (Colossians 3:5, ESV).

The collateral damage of the prosperity gospel movement is seen most evidently when its adherents learn that it leaves no meaningful room for pain and suffering in life. Followers of the movement often feel duped when life brings sickness, loss, and challenging circumstances. When you're not getting your return on investment from what you've "claimed by faith," it may appear as though Jesus isn't keeping up with His end of the bargain. The prosperity gospel avoids the commandment to pursue self-denial, mocking Christ's admonishment to 'take up your cross daily' and follow Him. Kyle Idleman said, "What you win them with is what you win them to."[11]

If people are drawn to Christ primarily because they expect Him to deliver material rewards, they are not truly being won to Christ Himself but to the benefits they believe He will supply. Jesus said those who wanted to be followers of Him must count the cost before making their decision. When we agree to count the cost, live in truth, and abide in Christ in authentic discipleship, we obtain the peace that passes all understanding that refutes the false expectation of a struggle-free life.

Commonly found in partnership with the prosperity gospel is what some call *Easy Believism*. This is the doctrine that stresses the concept of faith but often rejects repentance, the necessity of baptism in Jesus' name, and an evidentiary infilling of the Spirit. In easy believe-ism, salvation is often explained using language like, "I've called on the name of Jesus; I believe in Jesus; I've welcomed Him into my heart, and I've confessed Him as my Lord and Savior." Nevertheless, obedience to the commandments from God detailed by the Apostles in the book of Acts is often rejected in this movement.

These two sacred cows illustrate what happens when those professing to be Christians become the idols that they worship. In both cases, there is a disregard for the cost of discipleship, a resistance toward pain and suffering, and a willing ignorance toward the scriptures, all in an effort to get what we want when we want it. These doctrines are cheap, shallow, and unbiblical. Those who live by them can't see the immense and unimaginable cost of what Jesus did for us at Calvary, and without that realization it is impossible to see your sinful condition.

Some who embrace certain strands of prosperity teaching develop a distorted view of repentance and forgiveness. Though they might never say it aloud, the underlying attitude often comes across as, "If I do not have to repent to Jesus, then I do not have to repent to others either." This mindset shows itself in relationships. For example, when someone has absorbed a version of the prosperity gospel that focuses on blessing without transformation, they may expect forgiveness, trust, and reconciliation from those they have wronged without demonstrating genuine repentance. In some cases, individuals have even implied, "Jesus forgives me, so you have to forgive me," as if divine pardon automatically obligates others to restore the relationship. This turns forgiveness into a kind of emotional leverage, pressuring the offended party to move on while leaving the underlying harm unaddressed.

Can the Genuinely Converted Construct Idols?

Taking this a step further, could we be guilty of constructing our own golden calf, even if we've repented of our sins, been baptized in Jesus' name, and received the gift of the Holy Ghost? In short, yes! In the Exodus story, the Israelites are the chosen people of God; nevertheless, their chosen-ness did not prevent them from constructing an idol. Likewise, the church can be found guilty of building idols in the name of God. What is started in the

Spirit, ends in the flesh (Galatians 3:3) if we trade truth for compromise. It is important to remember that obvious forms of idolatry are not the only kind to be avoided. Sometimes, seemingly insignificant things can lead to unintended consequences. Addiction, ungodly relationships, and materialistic pursuits are problems that often appear easy to identify in life. However, there are others that are not as noticeable: Prioritizing personal entertainment, amusement, or employment over the things of God can become idols in the lives of people. The caveat here is that recreation, materials, and career are great and needful pursuits if they honor God and His Word. However, sometimes we can be found guilty of taking things that are good and honorable and shaping them into idols that God never intended us to have. Well-intentioned parents can even make idols of their children, living vicariously through their child's successes and focusing their attention on shaping their child in their own image. Whatever the idol, Psalms 115 offers a powerful warning about what idolatry will do to us.

> But our God is in the heavens: he hath done whatsoever he hath pleased. Their idols are silver and gold, the work of men's hands. They have mouths, but they speak not: eyes have they, but they see not: They have ears, but they hear not: noses have they, but they smell not: They have hands, but they handle not: feet have they, but they walk not: neither speak they through their throat. They that make them are like unto them; so is every one that trusteth in them. (Psalms 115:3-8, KJV)

The idol worshiper is as lifeless as the idol – spiritually blind, spiritually deaf, and spiritually mute. Those who worship worthless idols become worthless themselves (2 Kings 17:15).

We may not be guilty of propagating a particular sin or adhering to false doctrines like the prosperity gospel and easy believe-ism, but all have the capacity to stray away from God and generate their own "Golden Calf." Many are faithful in certain categories of godliness such as church attendance, giving, and fellowship yet remain in danger of becoming idolatrous. If we trust more in what we feel than what we know, our hearts will harden and we will find comfort in mixing truth with lies to appease our emotions. The result? Just as Israel reimagined their deliverance, claiming that an image made by their own hands delivered them out of Egypt, we can reimagine the story of our own deliverance, leaving Christ who redeemed us behind.

How Does This Show Up in the Church?

Like flies drawn to honey, so are flaws drawn to people. This is no different in the Church. Everyone is flawed. While human beings strive for perfection, we remain imperfect. Many begin their journey depending upon Jesus, only to turn to their own methods, preferences, and opinions by the end of it. By forgetting Who delivered us, we can fall prey to constructing our own religious ideas about who we believe saved us. There are many examples, but we will examine the following three:

1. Prioritizing the Past

2. Rules Before Relationship

3. Comfortable Compromise

Prioritizing the Past

Honoring and protecting history is necessary within the Church, but idolizing the past by thinking our best days are behind us is dangerous. Frequently viewing the past is wise, but looking forward takes precedence. When the present is challenging, it's easy to stare into the rear-view mirror. While grieving over what once was, we're blinded by how often "The good 'ole days are the combination of a bad memory and a good imagination."[12]

It is dangerous to value methods over the message or preferences over principles. We may cherish an older style of music that still holds beauty and meaning, but it was never the means of our salvation. Our methods, whether a change in music style, ministry programs, or other practices, must always align with the message of the gospel. The Body of Christ is not meant to be divided into cliques where each generation is isolated into its own group. Regardless of personal preference, we are called to be united in worshiping the Lord together in Spirit and in truth. When we elevate our preferences to the point of creating ultimatums, we are, in effect, giving them the kind of reverence and trust that belongs only to God, as if they were the very power that delivered us.

Rules Before Relationship

There's nothing wrong with effort. In fact, it's encouraged. We should labor with our brothers and sisters in Christ to reach our world. Nevertheless, expecting tenure in Christianity because of what we do makes us little different from those whom Jesus warned expected more blessing for time served (Matthew 20:9-14). Obedience that does not begin with relationship can lead to a sense of entitlement or an "I deserve" attitude. Jesus said, "If you love me, keep my commandments" (John 14:15). What we do flows from who we are in Christ. Viewing our lives in God as abiding by a checklist of 'dos and don'ts' (attempting to follow God's commands without a relationship with Him) leads us to exalt ourselves. Often, we compare our works with others, looking down on them so that we might feel better about ourselves. Rather than comparing ourselves with others, we will find that our righteousness never measures up to Christ. When we have an accurate view of humanity and a revelation of Jesus, we understand our merits, deeds, and successes did not bring us out of Egypt.

Comfortable Compromise

We are delivered out of the "House of Bondage" by the hand of God. We choose to come to Him in faith and repentance, but it is ultimately His undeserved grace that saves us. Some, however, treat conversion as a certificate of arrival, when in truth it is a birth certificate marking the start of a life of holiness and dependence on Jesus. Growth brings growing pains, and avoiding discomfort only stunts that growth. John Bevere points out that when Jesus said, "No man can come to me, except the Father which hath sent me draw him" (John 6:44, KJV), He was speaking about unbelievers being drawn to Him.[13]

Later, referring to His crucifixion, Jesus said, "And I, if I be lifted up from the earth, will draw all men unto me" (John 12:32, KJV). God draws the unbeliever to Himself, but as believers, it is our responsibility to determine our hunger for God, not His. We have the choice to submit to growing in relationship and spiritual maturity.

Failure to cultivate a daily relationship with God, maintain faithfulness to the Body of Christ, advance our love for Apostolic doctrine, and guard our hearts from offense leads to concession and compromise. Comfortable compromise, holding to certain biblical values while neglecting a true relationship with God, is a form of idolatry. For example, a Christian may ignore a holiness conviction because they have a loved one whose lifestyle is diametrically opposed to that conviction. Often, conviction is resisted on the grounds that one can still support the general moral teachings of the church and not obey other teachings about holiness. Still, without principles, convictions quickly fade into compromise. Many may attend church services regularly, give in the offering, and participate in worship, yet assimilate to the world around them in other areas of life. This behavior breeds confusion because of the dual identity. It also starts the clock on a ticking time-bomb of offense for that person because they will want the church to accommodate their dysfunction. Living a double life often causes people to expect others to affirm that double life – without that affirmation, offense comes quickly. What is sowed in the flesh is reaped in the flesh (Galatians 6:8). While consequences reaped by decisions of the flesh are often blamed on the church, such blame is insincere. Leaders who resist compromise are often characterized as problematic by those who would like to see the church conform to their own standard of living, rather than conforming themselves. Scapegoating the Church for their self-inflicted problems is very convenient as it acts as a smokescreen to keep them from looking within and addressing the real issues.

We have considered how refusing to grow in holiness, while complying in other areas such as church attendance, giving, and fellowship, falls into this trap of comfortable compromise. Another example is maintaining an outward

appearance of holiness that does not flow from an inti-
mate relationship with Christ or a genuine understanding
of Scripture. Just as rules without relationship can lead
to trouble in the life of a believer, so too can a divisive
attitude about holiness and separation. Without the right
spirit, holiness can become a pretext for cynicism and divi-
sion. Paul warned the church not to grieve the Spirit and
to: "Get rid of all bitterness, rage, anger, harsh words, and
slander, as well as all types of evil behavior. Instead, be kind
to each other, tenderhearted, forgiving one another, just as
God through Christ has forgiven you (Ephesians 4:31-
32, NLT). Joel Urshan once said, "Do not call yourself
Oneness if you claim one God but are dividing the body."[14]
Holiness and sanctification are inward works of the Spirit
that carry over in our attitude, behavior, and appearance.

The follower of Christ must remember that He is the
One who delivered you from sin and the world. Our idols
have not delivered us out of Egypt – to believe this is
self-deception and an example of forgetting the God who
delivered us.

Study Questions

1. Mixing Egypt with God doesn't work. In what ways have you tried to mix the world with Jesus? To that end, how did you justify your reasoning?

2. How has your family of origin impacted your view of God? Have there been areas of compromise (i.e., mixing truth with a lie) that were prominent?

3. What, if any, are the reasons many rely less on Jesus after they experience some form of deliverance?

4. If we have given our hearts to compromise, how can we untether ourselves from its grasp? In the process of turning back to God, what confrontations might we face in this decision?

Chapter 5:
In God We Trust

> *When we trust ourselves, we commit idolatry. When we commit idolatry, we conform to our idols. When we conform to our idols, we become enslaved to them. – Benjamin L. Gladd*

We live in a world where the expectation is not "What have you done for me?" but "What have you done for me lately?" We easily forget the kindness of others and the kindness of our Creator. In many ways, the culprit for this forgetfulness is misplaced trust. Each of us are either trusting in God or trusting in something else. Psalms 115 says, "Those who make idols *If you're not trusting God,* are just like them, as are all *you're forgetting God.* who trust in them." To trust in an idol is to construct your hope and security on a house of cards that is destined to collapse at the first sign of disturbance.

Our trust in Jesus isn't tested when everything is stable, but when we're thrown off balance by fear, unmet expectations, lack of fulfillment, difficult life challenges, and temptation to sin. Our allegiance is proven by what we cling to when life brings unwelcome disruptions. No matter the season, if you're not trusting God, you're forgetting God. Those who are soon to forget are soon to rebel. In rebellion, the exhilaration and awe of the miracles that occurred as little as days ago can dissipate into a faded memory. The plague of forgetfulness is littered throughout Scripture, but Psalms 106 effectively conveys how Israel repeatedly forgot:

> Our ancestors in Egypt were not impressed by the Lord's miraculous deeds. They soon forgot his many acts of kindness to them. Instead, they rebelled against him at the Red Sea. (Psalms 106:7, NLT)

> They traded their glorious God for a statue of a grass-eating bull. They forgot God, their savior, who had done such great things in Egypt. (Psalms 106:20-21, NLT)

> Then his people believed his promises. Then they sang his praise. Yet how quickly they forgot what he had done! They wouldn't wait for his counsel! In the wilderness, their desires ran wild, testing God's patience in that dry wasteland. (Psalms 106:12-14, NLT)

Disaster is imminent when we fail to remember God. These three passages reveal how forgetfulness nullifies the work of God in us by fueling impatience, rebellion, and idolatry. It is not enough to think we can ride high on His miraculous deeds of the past, but neglect to trust in Him. To experience genuine salvation while rejecting daily dependence on Jesus will fast-track you to spiritual dementia. In essence, if our trust in Him is absent today, our memory will fade – no matter how great the miracles of the past. The subtle nature of forgetfulness tempts us to rewrite history by filling in the vague memory gaps with whatever satisfies our desires in the present. The convert who neglects their walk with God and disconnects from the body of Christ has allowed forgetfulness to overcome their faithfulness.

How Fast Can You Forget God?

One month? Two months? How long does it take for someone to lose trust and forget about the goodness and mercy of Jesus? Israel complained about the bitter waters of Marah three days after victory at the Red Sea. So, the answer must be three days. "Right?" The better way to answer this question is with a question. We should ask ourselves, "How long does it take for my carnal appetite to return after God provides a victory?" Answering this question forces us to ask another: "What am I going to do about it?" Some break records seeking God for deliverance or receiving a miracle, but return their minds to Egypt once they have received what they want. Remember, when we are lost, we are not at war with our flesh because we are enslaved to it; once we have converted, the battle begins between flesh and Spirit, our carnal nature always fighting to usurp the governing Spirit of God in us.

This conflict of flesh against Spirit is epitomized by Israel's first battle following their 430-year Egyptian bondage. Amalek, their enemy, which becomes a thorn in the side of Israel for many generations, shares similarities with flesh. The opportunistic behavior and tactics of the Amalekites seem to resemble how our flesh attacks us. Notice, times of temptation often come when you face the acronym HALT (hungry, angry, lonely, tired).[15] However, we can also be tempted to sin when life is going well. Have you ever found yourself tempted in your flesh after a spiritual victory that left you feeling on top of the world? Has your old nature tried to capitalize on a God moment with sin? Flesh is insidious, tactical, and bold beyond belief. God has choice words for Amalek, what some may interpret as the representation of the enemy within us:

> Never forget what the Amalekites did to you as you came from Egypt. They attacked you when you were exhausted and weary, and they struck down those who were straggling behind. They had no fear of God. Therefore, when the Lord your God has given you rest from all your enemies in the land he is giving you as a special possession, you must destroy the Amalekites and erase their memory from under heaven. Never forget this! (Deuteronomy 25:17-19, NLT)

There is a part of us that does not fear God. As an opportunist lying in wait, this part seeks to take advantage of our deepest vulnerabilities and steal away our walk with God. Remember: "They that are Christ's have crucified the flesh with the affections and lusts. If we live in the Spirit, let us walk in the Spirit" (Galatians 5:24-25, KJV). The Apostle Paul encouraged Rome by sharing his own struggles in this regard. In many ways, Paul's struggle is encouraging because it is relatable:

> I have discovered this principle of life—that when I want to do what is right, I inevitably do what is wrong. I love God's law with all my heart. But there is another power within me that is at war with my mind. This power makes me a slave to the sin that is still within me. (Romans 7:21-23, NLT)

Paul was neither a hypocrite nor perfect in the war with his flesh. He learned that his own effort to win this war was futile because his will was never strong enough to sustain the victory. It is only by the Spirit of God that you can "put to death the deeds of your sinful nature" and be "led by the Spirit of God" (Romans 8:13-14). Paul admonished his readers to have the "mind of Christ"; at the same time, there is a war in the mind. Knowing what is right but making decisions that contradict your morality is an exhausting mental exercise. Hence, our memory will take on a "mind of its own" if our hearts and minds are not fixed on Christ.

Selective Memory

"We remember the fish we used to eat for free in Egypt.
And we had all the cucumbers, melons, leeks, onions, and gar-
lic we wanted. But now our appetites are gone. All we ever see
is this manna!" (Numbers 11:5-6, NLT)

After having manna for breakfast, lunch, and dinner for
a year, the miracle became monotonous to the people of
Israel. They began to loath the loaves and looked back to
the supposed benefits of living in Egypt. Their daydream-
ing became complaining as they murmured, "Oh, how
wonderful was the buffet we had in Egypt! All we have
now is this manna!" Notice, Israel did not complain about
the lack of provision; they complained about the lack of
variety. God was providing for them, but they wanted to
decide what was on the menu. Their palate for variety dic-
tated their decisions and manipulated their memory. "We
remember the fish we used to eat for free in Egypt!" It is a
contradiction in terms: "free in Egypt." They remembered
familiar pleasures but forgot the slavery, bondage, tyranny,
and suffering.

When we exaggerate our present situation, we often
romanticize the past. Selective memory, also known as
euphoric recall is a snare in which we can easily become
tangled. Just as Israel looked at Egypt through rose-col-
ored glass, we must not alter the truth of the memory of
our Egypt. To embellish the past and think sin wasn't so

bad, forgetting the bondage that accompanied it, we minimize and justify our decision to fulfill a carnal appetite. These moments lead to a fork in the road: (1) Often, we forget the reality of the goodness of God and the

If we exaggerate our present situation, we will romanticize the past.

reality of the wickedness of life in sin. (2) Even in moments of powerful temptation, we must look to trust in Jesus and find fulfillment that only comes through Him.

For some of us, eating pizza two days in a row is too much. What's wrong with Israel saying, "Hey, we've had this same meal for a year; it would be nice to have something different." For Israel, the problem was not the foods listed from Egypt, it was the delusion that what was in the past was better than what God provided. Israel rejected God's provision, failing to see His promise of the future that flowed with milk and honey (Exodus 13:5). In Numbers chapter fourteen, Israel's lack of daily trust in God led to unbelief, and that unbelief kept them from entering the promised land of Canaan.

As a result, they spent forty years in the wilderness, learning to depend on Him for their needs each day. Sometimes what feels like walking in circles spiritually is actually a season when God is teaching us the same lesson—how to rely on Him. The wilderness is not just a place of testing; it's a place of preparation. Trust in God isn't only for the hard seasons, it's also for the blessings ahead. Even when we have learned dependence on God, it doesn't mean we will graduate to self-sustainment. The way He provides may change from one season to another, but our need for Him never changes. Jesus said, "I am the bread of life: he that cometh to me shall never hunger; and he that believeth on me shall never thirst" (John 6:35, KJV). The Lord's prayer includes, "Give us this day our daily bread" (Matthew 6:11). Our provision is Jesus. What a blessed life to feast on His Word, be filled with His Spirit, and live in daily relationship with Him. Every child of God can testify of how He provided miraculously. Examples include how "He put food on the table when we couldn't make ends meet. The doctor's report wasn't in my favor, but God stepped in when all signs pointed toward despair. My marriage was broken to pieces as fine as dust, yet somehow Jesus mended the covenant that was shattered."

Testimony after testimony proves God's provision. Nevertheless, much like Israel, we can find ourselves forgetting all that the Lord has done for us. We might ask ourselves the question, "How do we arrive at a place where living for God appears difficult or mundane?" Remember: if you neglect the bread of life, your palate will gravitate toward nourishment from the past. When the provision of God becomes "old" to you, looking towards the buffet of options in Egypt reveals the despising of the Daily Bread.

Prayer: Remembering in Practice

Nothing helps us remember God like prayer. Prayers of repentance remind us of our destructive tendencies and our desperate need for forgiveness. As we offer prayers of praise, we recall to memory who He is, affirming gratitude. Prayers of petition remind us of all He's done for us, encouraging us to place our faith and trust in the One who knows best. If prayer is remembering in practice, we can presume those who have forgotten God are those who've detached themselves from prayer.

Once life begins to stabilize, it's easy for us to push God to the margins, as if His presence was only necessary during our crisis rather than essential every step of the way. Using prayer as a means to an end misaligns the purpose of prayer and is a surefire way to fail. Humans pray the most when we've exhausted all other resources in distress. Often, when the trouble is gone, so is our prayer life. It is a shame when church leadership shows more concern for us after we have received our victory than when we are suffering yet earnestly seeking God.

Dark times draw us to our knees. It has been said that there are no atheists in foxholes. In many ways, this summarizes many people's attitude toward prayer. In treating God like the Father we only come to when we need something we miss out on the greater part of relationship. We might ask ourselves, "How does my absence in prayer grieve the heart of God?"

Maybe you're reading this and wondering if any of it applies to you. Perhaps you recognize that your motives for prayer are not entirely pure. Even so, thank God you are praying. The very act of turning to God, even imperfectly, can be the beginning of deeper repentance, refinement, and relationship. Through prayer, God can transform you and your motives. It is discovered in prayer that Jesus may not change your circumstances the way you envisioned, but He can do the most important work of changing you.

Sometimes, we pray to address problems in life that we have created. Other times, we pray to address problems that life brings to us. Stan Gleason once recalled a difficulty he experienced as a young man. In his retelling, he shared words from his father that gave him encourage-

Don't ever disparage anything that makes you want to pray.

ment in his struggle: "Don't ever disparage anything that makes you want to pray."[16] Although we don't know what motivated his plea, Paul asked God three times for the "thorn in his flesh" to be removed, yet the thorn was not removed (2 Corinthians 12:8). Instead, the Lord granted him grace that would sustain him. The thorn humbled Paul, lest he would be exalted above measure and caused him to rejoice in that it forced him to rely on the grace

IN GOD WE TRUST

of God (2 Corinthians 12:7-10). It was in his weakness that Paul found strength in God. The paradox of despising and rejoicing happens when we discover the purpose of the pain that brings us into fellowship with our Savior. In Philippians, often called the book of joy, Paul said: "That I may know him, and the power of his resurrection, and the fellowship of his sufferings, being made conformable unto his death;" (Philippians 3:10). As we come to know God through prayer, we understand like Paul that our thorn is a light affliction compared to the crown of thorns that was upon His head, the nails that were in His hands and feet, and the sins of the world that were upon His shoulders.

Ingratitude: Lurking in Selective Memory

"You should know this, Timothy, that in the last days there will be very difficult times. For people will love only themselves and their money. They will be boastful and proud, scoffing at God, disobedient to their parents, and ungrateful."
— (2 Timothy 3:1-2, NLT)

Included in Paul's list of serious offenses, he included the sins of ungratefulness and un-thankfulness. While it may appear trivial to some, ingratitude contributes to selective memory of the past and drives us to murmur, complain, doubt, and walk in unbelief. "Be careful for nothing; but in every thing by prayer and supplication with thanksgiving let your requests be made known unto God" (Philippians 4:6, KJV). Being thankful, even in the most dire of situations, must be found in our prayers. One might rightly wonder, am I supposed to be thankful in seasons of grieving and pain? Am I supposed to thank God for my affliction? Still, remember that Paul did not say to be thankful *for* affliction, but to be thankful *in* affliction (1 Thessalonians 5:18).

Consider when a believer becomes sick. The example of the New Testament is not to become jaded or sarcastic, reminding God insincerely that we are thankful for sickness. Rather, in the heaviness, our prayers should, perhaps, sound like this; "Thank you, Jesus, for your sovereign hand in my suffering. I pray for your guidance and leading. Everything in me wants to get out of this, but I ask for you to show me what I can get out of this. Mold me! Shape me! I ask for healing in your name but above all else, I'm thankful for the redemption in my life and the daily relationship I have with you by your mercy and grace." Even in trials, Paul, writing from prison, said, "And the peace of God, which passeth all understanding, shall keep your hearts and minds through Christ Jesus" (Philippians 4:7, KJV).

Study Questions

1. What are some attitudes and actions that reveal our lack of trust and gratitude in the daily provision of God?

2. Why is it that we go through the cycle of drawing close to God when we are in a crisis only to pull back after our storm has calmed? Could it be we are placing ourselves in an endless cycle of dysfunction because we're not learning to depend on Jesus in every season?

Chapter 6:
Blinded by the
gods Before Me

| *Thou shalt have no other gods before me.* — (*Exodus 20:3, KJV*)

Is there ever a time for deception? Would a little lie for the greater good, even if impermissible, still be understandable? Bending and avoiding the truth to prevent someone from feeling pain is a powerful temptation. We think we protect others and especially ourselves by refusing to acknowledge hard truths; all the while, our avoidance gives way to wasted time, unaddressed shame, and the slow descent into self-deception. Choosing to reject what is true is more than just turning a blind eye – it is opening the door to lies and spiritual blindness, giving them place in our hearts. Deception dulls our sensitivity to Jesus, who is the way, the truth, and the life (John 14:6). Paul said, "In whom the god of this world hath blinded the minds of them which believe not, lest the light of the glorious gospel of Christ, who is the image of God, should shine unto them" (2 Corinthians 4:4, KJV). By believing and applying the truth of God's word, no matter how painful, the light of God breaks through the darkness that has made us spiritually blind.

No matter the circumstance, truth is always the right path. As Jamie Buckingham cleverly titled his book, *The Truth Will Set You Free, but First It Will Make You Miserable*, truth often begins with discomfort. The path may start difficult, but the result is freedom in Christ. Willful deception will enslave you when delusion is chosen over truth. Being miserable for a season to be made whole sounds a lot better than being satisfied in a lie and enslaved. For example, some individuals who abuse drugs are using a numbing agent to enable them to avoid the hard reality of their brokenness. Much like the prodigal son of Luke fifteen, it is often in the midst of the consequences of the pigpen that you come to yourself, assess the damage you've caused, and decide whether to return to the Father. In many cases, when an addict becomes sober, they feel the full impact of their choices that were before unfelt due to living in the darkness of deception. Truth is hard. However, in the story of the prodigal son, his repentance led him back to a father who was ready to embrace and restore him. Coming to yourself – no longer believing the lies that your sin is not that bad and repenting – is a process that can be painful, but it is the path to freedom and forgiveness from our Father.

A.W. Tozer said, "The hardest deception to cure is that which is self-imposed."[17] Performing mental gymnastics to preserve personal viewpoint over truth does not keep danger out; instead, it is like building a prison to house our shame, avoidance, and fear.

> *The hardest deception to cure is that which is self-imposed – A.W. Tozer*

In many cases, self-deception begins when we place idols we have created between ourselves and God. The book of Exodus commanded the Israelites to have no other gods *before* Him. The reader may notice that the commandment does not say, "Thou shalt have no other gods *above* me." Our sin breaks God's heart because it separates us from Him. It not only impacts our relationship with God, but also our vision of God. We can't see the goodness and majesty of God because we can't see through our idol(s) that we position between us and Christ! If an idol stands between us and our God, our perception becomes blurred, as lies impede our vision of truth. J. Alec Motyer said, "The idolater chose a delusion and became deluded."[18] Paul shows us this path we must avoid in Romans 1:20-25:

- *20* – God is clearly seen through His Creation.
- *21* – Those who choose not to worship Him construct foolish ideas about Him. Thus, their minds become dark and confused.
- *22* – They believe they're wise, but they're fools.
- *23* – They worshiped idols instead of God.

- *24* – God gave them over to their own desires because…
- *25* – They chose to exchange truth for a lie and worship creation over creator.

Generations in the Darkness of Self-Deception

Avoiding reality leads one to spiritual darkness and sends them into the pain of being separated from Jesus. Like horse blinders, we can focus on what we want so much that we don't consider the path we're taking to get there. When we see our idol instead of our God, our destination is always a rude awakening. Sadly, our idolatry often affects others as well. It is incumbent upon us to keep our attention on the God before us and to remove the idols that stand in our path.

Spiritual blindness can have a generational impact. In some cases, fathers may become so consumed by the demands of work, believing they are providing well for their families, that they unintentionally drift into a subtle form of idolatry. The pursuit of provision, though noble, can sometimes overshadow devotion to God and connection with the body of believers. This is not to say that all hard-working fathers are spiritually blind or materialistic. Many sacrifice deeply and rightly in service to their families. However, when work becomes a substitute for worship, or when financial security is prioritized over spiritual leadership, the next generation often inherits the benefits of provision but also the consequences of misplaced priorities. While in many cases secular culture resists the notion that time should be set aside for God, it is apparent from the scriptures that believers have a responsibility to do so. Secularism does not share the priorities of the church. Work schedules, sporting events, and social activities are often held on Sundays, disregarding the time that is normally set aside for God. When the fabric of faithfulness to God and family is broken, idolatry is likely to abound.

Spiritual blindness often has downstream effects. Parents who allow fear and worry to consume their lives can pass this same behavior on to their children. Yet, Paul wrote to Timothy, "For God hath not given us the spirit of fear, but of power and of love and of a sound mind" (2 Timothy 1:7, KJV). Often, purpose in life goes unfulfilled because fear of the future paralyzes us.

Sometimes we forget that parents were once children who likely encountered circumstances that were unjust. However, if a parent has endured any form of childhood trauma, they must tear down the "idol of avoidance" and turn with honesty toward God. There are some situations that may necessitate seeking professional help in order to walk through the pain that will not resolve itself on its own. If not, they will be unable to lead their family because their wounds cloud their vision. Pain is either transformed or transmitted, and many times, children shoulder the burden of unaddressed issues in their parents. Untreated toxic patterns in one generation can become the momentum that starts the domino effect of passing dysfunction and disorder to the next. However, when we choose to be the domino that does not fall, we take on the inertia of all the other ones that did. When we say, "It stops with me," we are choosing to look to truth over self-deception, arduous work over avoidance, and navigate scripturally through our pain rather than numbing it.

Proverbs 29:18 says, "Where there is no vision, the people perish." The right path is only seen when there is nothing standing between you and Jesus.

How Could I Be So Blind?

The saying, "You Don't Know What You Don't Know," feels like an oversimplification of our lack of know-how in certain areas of life. As adults, the gaps in our thinking occasionally come from inexperience in our formative years. Circumstances might seem normal to some, but foreign to us because our upbringing lacked necessary leadership. Parents who are spiritually blind trying to lead children who do not know any better themselves is like the blind leading the blind. Some might wonder: "How am I supposed to parent when I was not properly parented? How am I supposed to be a spiritual leader when much of my life was void of godly examples? How am I to see with clarity when I don't even know where my vision is impaired?" The answer is simple: conversion and discipleship combat spiritual blindness. Conversion shines the light of God into darkness and begins the journey of being a disciple of Jesus. Discipleship is the ongoing process of following Jesus, gradually allowing the scales to fall from our eyes. When we are discipled, we overcome self-deception, carnal defaults, and our false perceptions of God and His Church.

Countering Spiritual Blindness Through Discipleship

In the Gospels, Israel was blind because of their unbelief, prioritizing their religion over relationship. Even the disciples of Jesus, who witnessed His miracles firsthand, could not seem to grasp a full understanding of who He was due to cultural blinders affecting their perception. They sometimes missed the obvious, lacked faith, and misunderstood the purpose of Jesus. Many failed to see Him as the Messiah who would go to the cross. Instead, they wanted Him to be their liberator from Roman tyranny. While many who opposed Jesus saw Him as a miracle man, those closest to Him often saw Him through the lens of their selfish agenda as well. They looked at the Truth, yet they could not see Him for who He was. We must learn the same lesson the people of the first century learned: Instead of viewing Jesus through our personal bias and experience, we must see Him for who He is.

In Mark eight, Jesus gives us a masterclass of three steps to combat spiritual blindness. First, Jesus illustrated the spiritual blindness of the disciples by using a literal blind man as an example:

> When they arrived at Bethsaida, some people brought a blind man to Jesus, and they begged him to touch the man and heal him. Jesus took the blind man by the hand and led him out of the village. Then, spitting on the man's eyes, he laid his hands on him and asked, "Can you see anything now?" The man looked around. "Yes," he said, "I see people, but I can't see them very clearly. They look like trees walking around." Then Jesus placed his hands on the man's eyes again, and his eyes were opened. His sight was completely restored, and he could see everything clearly. Jesus sent him away, saying, "Don't go back into the village on your way home." (Mark 8:22-26, NLT)

It is the opinion of the writer that the point of this healing is not that Jesus made a mistake the first time that required a second attempt. Rather, this healing was a message to the disciples, illustrating how their spiritual blindness would be healed gradually. The disciples were like this man whose vision went from blind, to blurry, to finally clear. If the disciples, who were with Jesus, were in a progressive process of having their understanding opened, how much more should we remain faithful in discipleship? Our walk with Christ is a lifelong undertaking, and it progressively opens our understanding to the truth of God and the misguided confidence of our understanding.

After Jesus compared the twelve to this blind man, Simon Peter had an exchange with Jesus that reveals the healing that can occur through discipleship: revelation, self-examination, and self-denial.

Step 1: Revelation

Jesus and His disciples left Galilee and went up to the villages near Caesarea Philippi. As they were walking along, he asked them, "Who do people say I am?" "Well," they replied, "some say John the Baptist, some say Elijah, and others say you are one of the other prophets." Then he asked them, "But who do you say I am?" Peter replied, "You are the Messiah." (Mark 8:27-29, NLT)

Peter proclaimed Jesus to be the Messiah. In fact, Jesus praised him by saying, "Blessed art thou, Simon Barjona: for flesh and blood hath not revealed it unto thee, but my Father which is in heaven. And I say also unto thee, That thou art Peter, and upon this rock I will build my church; and the gates of hell shall not prevail against it" (Matthew 16:17-18, KJV). What a moment for Peter! He states his revelation of the identity of Christ, is lauded publicly, and then Jesus states the identity and purpose of Peter. However, his emotional pinnacle was short-lived. Like many of us, Peter's revelation of Christ was incomplete. We may have a revelation of Jesus, but that doesn't mean that

Peering at Jesus through the lens of the Word of God is the prescription to take us from blurry to clear vision.

our revelation is complete. Having an experience with God does not mean we are not viewing Him through the lens of our own personal bias and need a prescription for our abstract view. When we only look at Jesus through the lens of what we want Him to be, our vision becomes blurred. If we are willing to look at Jesus through the corrective lens of the Word of God, our vision of Him will become clear.

What is the danger in having blurry vision? As we'll discover, Simon Peter's next short-sighted decision caused him to take a nosedive from his emotional high of revelation to the emotional low of rebuke.

Step 2: Self-Examination

Then Jesus began to tell them that the Son of Man must suffer many terrible things and be rejected by the elders, the leading priests, and the teachers of religious law. He would be killed, but three days later he would rise from the dead. As he talked about this openly with his disciples, Peter took him aside and began to reprimand him for saying such things. Jesus turned around and looked at his disciples, then reprimanded Peter. "Get away from me, Satan!" he said. "You are seeing things merely from a human point of view, not from God's." (Mark 8:31-33, NLT)

Two questions come to mind: why would Peter reprimand Jesus, and how did he have the gall to do so? First, his rebuke of Jesus was rooted in his own lack of understanding of who the Messiah would be. Hearing of suffering and death did not match up with Peter's understanding that Jesus would be the conquering king, vindicating Israel. As Jesus said, Peter saw from a human point of view and not God's. Human understanding rejects a crucified Christ because we don't want to identify with suffering. Human understanding has no problem seeing Jesus as healer and deliverer, but it resists knowing Him as the suffering servant because we don't want to identify with a suffering servant ourselves. If we look at Jesus with human understanding, we will reject God for who He is, abdicate our responsibility in identifying with Him, and attempt to wield God as we wish. When we refuse to see Jesus in His entirety, we will fill in the gaps of His identity with what we desire.

Further, we cannot dismiss Peter's revelation of Jesus, because it came from God. While at one time in his life, revelation happened to Peter, revelation did not prevent him from misunderstanding Christ at a later time. Again, the problem lies in how he viewed this revelation through the filter of his human point of view. Those who rely on revelation alone are often overconfident in their interpretation of God's Word. Peter's overconfidence revealed that he didn't see the full picture; for Simon Peter, it sounded like this: "Jesus, I heard from God, and you don't know what you're talking about." You know your perception is skewed when you are trying to correct God. Peter couldn't see that his actions contradicted the scriptures and the spiritual authority that was over him. We should ask ourselves how we have behaved similarly. In what ways have we ignored spiritual leadership because we thought we knew what God wanted, when, in reality, it was what we wanted?

Peter is one example of how a sincere heart, coupled with bad thinking, can lead to disaster.[19] As the saying goes, "The road to hell is paved with good intentions." Peter believed he was operating in love by rebuking God in the flesh. He unwittingly did the work of Satan by discouraging Jesus from going to the cross. Although unaware of his actions, Peter went from being a messenger of God to a messenger of Satan. Much like Peter, we can become a messenger of Satan, even unwittingly, when we are motivated by love without truth. In this way, many believe they are serving God when, in reality, they are servants of Satan. This is, perhaps, the greatest delusion of all.

Here is Peter, who, in one moment, is given a powerful foreshadowing of his calling, to the next being called "Satan." Jesus showed Peter that his private intentions had devilish results. Like Simon Peter, our perception needs correction when we veer away from the Word of God. Much like Peter, we often need rebuke; this is an act of love that God performs on our behalf. When corrected by the word of God through spiritual leadership and godly examples, we can either resist or submit. Rather than viewing correction as an attack, it should be understood as love in action. "For whom the Lord loveth he correcteth; even as a father the son in whom he delighteth" (Proverbs 3:12 KJV). When we encounter the loving correction of God's Word, it's worth asking ourselves questions like these: "What am I missing here? Could it be that I'm not seeing the big picture? Am I allowing myself to become offended? How can I respond in a way that pleases God?"

When confronted with their failures, hardened hearts rebel, but humbled hearts desire to see truth.

Step 3: Self-Denial

Then, calling the crowd to join his disciples, he said, "If any of you wants to be my follower, you must give up your own way, take up your cross, and follow me. If you try to hang on to your life, you will lose it. But if you give up your life for my sake and for the sake of the Good News, you will save it. And what do you benefit if you gain the whole world but lose your own soul? Is anything worth more than your soul? If anyone is ashamed of me and my message in these adulterous and sinful days, the Son of Man will be ashamed of that person when he returns in the glory of his Father with the holy angels." (Mark 8:34-38, NLT)

Interestingly, Jesus closes this passage with a portrait of His crucifixion and our participation in the same. Jesus told His disciples to deny themselves, take up their cross, and follow Him. Not only would He not ask us to do something that He wouldn't do, but our affliction is nothing compared to the suffering He endured. Jesus died for us so that we could die to our flesh and live through Him. Jesus bore the weight of the world on His shoulders – because of this, our "yoke is easy and burden is light" (Matthew 11:30).

Following Jesus the way He intended does not lead to resentment. There is joy in serving Him daily. Softened hearts allow the Word of God and the Spirit to show us His plan. We glorify Him by serving others. This plan includes seeing Christ for who He is and not for what we want Him to be. To deny ourselves is to do everything in our power to remove any false god that is before us. No matter what it takes, we will not let idol worship stand between us and Christ. He is the One True God – not a construct of our flawed human point of view. We must see Him as Savior and Lord as well as King and Suffering Servant.

Suffering and resurrection go together. They are knit together in the life of the child of God. Paul writes with complete clarity the joy of the Lord he experienced in the deepest of suffering. He says, "I want to know Christ and experience the mighty power that raised him from the dead. I want to suffer with him, sharing in his death, so that one way or another I will experience the resurrection from the dead" (Philippians 3:10-11, NLT). By sharing in the fellowship of His suffering, we also share in the power of His resurrection.

Study Questions

1. The Path of Choice flow chart shows the avenues we choose to take after we have been tempted/deceived and sin. Can you identify a time when you were in the right column of descending into darkness? What decisions did you make that brought you there and how did it feel?

2. At what moment was the light switch flipped on which began the process of coming out of spiritual darkness?

The Path of Choice

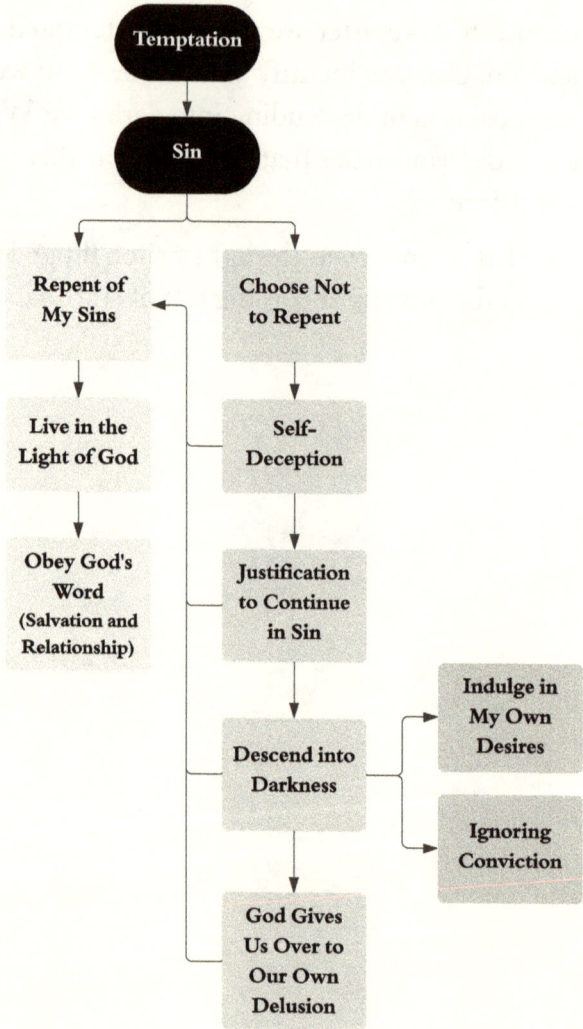

```
        ┌──────────────┐
        │  Temptation  │
        └──────┬───────┘
               ↓
        ┌──────────────┐
        │     Sin      │
        └──────┬───────┘
```

Repent of My Sins	Choose Not to Repent
Live in the Light of God	Self-Deception
Obey God's Word (Salvation and Relationship)	Justification to Continue in Sin
	Descend into Darkness
	God Gives Us Over to Our Own Delusion

Indulge in My Own Desires

Ignoring Conviction

Chapter 7:
You Choose Your Legacy

God makes it clear that when the parents choose to turn from him and pursue idols, their children will experience a bending, twisting, and distortion in their lives. — Jan Silvious[20]

We are not held accountable for the sins of our parents or others, but we are affected by them. In her book, *"Please Don't Say You Need Me: Biblical Answers for Codependency,"* Jan Silvious identifies how many battle to be free from their parents' idolatry. They say things like:

- My father was an alcoholic. (His idol was alcohol.)

- My mother ran around on my father. (Her idol was promiscuous behavior.)

- My father beat my mother and she just kept taking it. (Her idol was the "security" of having a husband.)

- My mother left us when we were children to live with another man. (Her idol was her own pleasure and security.)

- My father was hooked on drugs and many nights we had no food. (His idol was drugs.)

In every case, the parents were caught in an obsession with alcohol, drugs, another person, or themselves, and the children were left to cope with the "visitation of iniquity" in their own lives. In the Old Testament Hebrew, the word for iniquity literally means "perversion." It comes from a root word, *awon*, that means to "bend, twist, or distort."

Following the command to have "No other gods before me," the Lord shows us how this bending, twisting, and distortion of idolatry harms a legacy. He says,

> Thou shalt not make unto thee any graven image, or any likeness of any thing that is in heaven above, or that is in the earth beneath, or that is in the water under the earth. Thou shalt not bow down thyself to them, nor serve them: for I the Lord thy God am a jealous God, visiting the iniquity of the fathers upon the children unto the third and fourth generation of them that hate me. (Exodus 20:4-5, KVJ)

The phrase, "visitation of iniquity," highlights the concept of generational consequences of sin. This does not imply that children are punished for their parents' sins, but the consequences of sin can have lasting effects. Ezekiel 18:20 clarifies that each person is responsible for their own sin, yet the environment and patterns set by previous generations can influence future ones.[21] The impact of idolatry on the next generation is revealed in many ways, such as:

1. Children are especially vulnerable to adopting the idolatry of their closest influencers because they perceive
   their environment, no matter how toxic, as normal
   and familiar. The distorted thought patterns cultivated
   in an idolatrous atmosphere can lead them to accept
   and even become comfortable living in a spiritually
   broken state.

2. Idolatry, by its very nature, is the antithesis of love,
   compelling us to seek fulfillment in all the wrong
   places. As discussed in Chapter Six, idols obstruct our
   vision of God, distorting our understanding of who
   He is. This distortion is especially evident in the way
   children perceive God through the lens of their parents, particularly their father. When a father is absent,
   neglectful, or abusive, a child may internalize a false
   perception that God is distant and unloving. Rather
   than filling that void with the One who embodies
   perfect love, there is a temptation to seek validation
   elsewhere. If a key figure in one's life has abandoned
   them in any capacity, unresolved anger and resentment
   may be projected onto God, the One who promises
   never to leave or forsake us.

As inheritors of either a legacy of righteousness or
unrighteousness, we hold the power to determine the kind
of legacy we leave behind. Whether we choose to perpetu-
ate a legacy of idolatry or one of faithful service to God is a

decision that rests in our hands. While the sins of parents can negatively impact multiple generations, God's love and mercy extend far beyond those consequences. This is expressed in the next verse of our passage from Exodus: "And shewing mercy unto thousands of them that love me, and keep my commandments" (Exodus 20:6, KJV). To keep His commandments and abide in Christ is to participate in His enduring faithfulness that reaches us and blesses generations after us.

Put Away the "Old" gods of Egypt

Although the distortion, twisting, and bending have been thrust upon the mind and heart of succeeding generations because of the sins of the parents, each of us still has individual responsibility to know the truth and straighten our thinking. – Jan Silvious[xxi]

While standing in the Promised Land, Joshua commanded Israel to make a choice about who they would serve. He urged them, saying, "Put away the gods which your fathers served on the other side of the flood, and in Egypt; and serve ye the Lord" (Joshua 24:14). His message was clear: do not let the gods your fathers served become your gods!

Though we may have been dealt an unfair hand in life, one shaped by the choices and influences of those before us, it remains our responsibility to put away the idols that have been passed down to us. We must confront the hard truth and acknowledge where we have sinned by our own volition, regardless of external influences. True transformation begins when we take ownership of our actions and obey God. Jan Silvious provides another powerful example of what it means to take responsibility. She emphasizes how those seeking healing from idolatrous dependency issues begin the journey of true recovery by acknowledging personal responsibility. Silvious highlights that lasting change requires confronting the root of these dependencies. She says,

> I personally believe that if people understand why they feel, think, and react the way they do, then they can counter their thoughts with truth. If I tell a man or woman, "You are emotionally dependent because of the idolatry of your father," and then I say, "Bless your heart," excusing their sinful behavior, I have failed to offer help and hope. But if I say, "You are emotionally dependent because of the idolatry of your father, and it's sinful for you to remain dependent. But there is a way out," then I have given them information that can lead to change.[22]

Our twisted thinking is straightened by the hard work of pursuing truth and taking responsibility. Renouncing the idolatrous attachments stemming from our upbringing and choosing to pursue God by practicing the biblical definition of forgiveness are just a few key components of the journey to wholeness. But how do we navigate situations in which we bear the consequences of another's actions? The answer is clear: regardless of what others choose, we must remain faithful to God.

Numbers chapter fourteen offers a striking example of unwavering faithfulness through the story of Joshua and Caleb, who stood firm when others faltered in unbelief. After exploring the Promised Land, ten of the twelve spies returned, spreading fear like a contagion. This wave of unbelief swept through the nation, manifesting in fear-mongering, complaints, threats to return to Egypt, and a call to stone Joshua and Caleb. Despite the rebellion, these two men remained resolute. Their faithfulness was undeterred by the unfaithfulness that surrounded them, demonstrating how true commitment to God continues, even when tested by the fear and doubt of others. Furthermore, it was when Israel tried to silence the faith of Joshua and Caleb that God stepped in.

Israel's faithlessness caused the generation that left Egypt to be denied entry into the Promised Land. Instead of entering Canaan, that generation wandered the wilderness for forty years until they passed away. During this time, Joshua and Caleb, the faithful two, were preserved so that they could enter and possess the land when the others could not. We find that the faithful are preserved and prepared for the promise even through the refining crucible of the wilderness.

Preservation – After forty years in the wilderness, every man of fighting age who had left Egypt perished, except Joshua and Caleb. Caleb's words testify to God's sustaining power: "I am as strong now as I was when Moses sent me on that journey, and I can still travel and fight as well as I could then" (Joshua 14:11, NLT). God honors commitment by granting the strength to endure any circumstance. Though in many ways we might bear the consequences of others' actions, God never forgets us. Even when life feels unfair, faithfulness shields our hearts from bitterness and unforgiveness. As we grow older, faithfulness strengthens our spiritual walk. We are assured that God remembers and rewards those who remain faithful, for He is faithful.

Preparation – Faithfulness is the foundation of leadership. Joshua succeeded Moses, leading Israel into Canaan after forty years. It was Joshua who commanded the Israelites to put away their idols. Joshua trusted in God from Egypt through the wilderness. Seasons of unfairness and wilderness wandering are not wasted; they are the proving grounds where trust in God is forged. It is in these moments that integrity is refined, enabling you to stand firm and lead others with confidence.

Promise – At eighty-five years old, Caleb said, "So give me the hill country that the Lord promised me" (Joshua 14:12, NLT). The promise of entering the land of Canaan gave him the joy to endure the wilderness season. Notice,

Caleb didn't just endure the wilderness – he emerged with a conquering spirit. At an age when most would hang up their swords and settle into retirement, Caleb refused to let his faith grow weary. He didn't limp into the land of promise; he ran in to "capture mountains and conquer giants!"[23] As faithful children of God, we too press on toward the promises of eternity, even when the wilderness tries to wear us down. And when we emerge, others don't just hear our testimonies; they witness our *follow-through faith*. Warren Wiersbe captures the generational impact of "Caleb-like" faith when he says:

> In Joshua 15:13–19, we see Caleb providing for the next generation. Some of Caleb's daring faith rubbed off on his son-in-law Othniel, who later became a judge in the land (Judg. 3:7–11). Caleb's faith also touched his daughter, for she had the faith to ask her father for a field and then for springs of water to irrigate the land. Caleb's example of faith was more valuable to his family than the property he claimed for them.

Don't Take on the New gods of Canaan

> And if it seem evil unto you to serve the Lord, choose you this day whom ye will serve; whether the gods which your fathers served that were on the other side of the flood, or the gods of the Amorites, in whose land ye dwell: but as for me and my house, we will serve the Lord. (Joshua 24:15, KJV)

Tragedy unfolds after this passage in Joshua. Scripture paints a heartbreaking picture of Israel's constant vacillation between serving God and serving idols, often

attempting the impossible task of doing both. After step-
ping into the land of promise, they did exactly what God
had commanded them not to do; they embraced the gods
of Canaan: Baal, Molech, and Ashtoreth. They didn't just
bow before the idols; they gave Molech the ultimate offering, sacrificing their own children in fire. This is the epitome
of a generational collapse caused by disobedience and
idolatry. Nevertheless, before we cast judgment on ancient
Israel, we must confront an unsettling truth: modern-day
idolatry leaves its own trail of devastation. While no one
today burns their children on literal altars, many families
unknowingly offer their children to different idols—success, achievement, and approval. Many tell themselves it
is for their child's future, as they push them toward endless activities, accolades, and academic excellence, all while
neglecting to nurture a heart that beats for God.

In trading spiritual formation for worldly success, we
risk the same kind of generational loss Israel suffered.
Just as the faithless generation was denied entry into
the Promised Land, many of today's children are at risk
of missing the eternal inheritance God desires for them.
The urgent question remains: What altars are we building
for our children, and what promises might they forfeit in
the process?

The question is sobering: How many altars have we
built in our homes that lead our children away from God?

What are we really offering them to? Let us not repeat Israel's tragic pattern because the legacy we leave will be determined by who or what we choose to serve.

There's a clarion call to put away the old gods and don't take on any new ones. God is calling us to put down our idols, and He has assured us that He will be with us every step of the way. We are not left to do this alone. We can walk forward with confidence because "He who began a good work in you will carry it on to completion until the day of Jesus Christ" (Philippians 1:6).

Not One, But Two Golden Calves

There is no shortage of new gods vying for our devotion, many of which lie beyond the scope of this book. But there is one more I want to address: the idol of "Convenient Christianity."

Many years after Joshua's passing, there arose a king in Israel named Solomon. At one time in his life, Solomon was the epitome of wisdom; nevertheless, he became foolish by embracing the idols of his wives and concubines. They turned his heart from God, and he worshiped Ashtoreth, Milcom, Chemosh, and Molech (1 Kings 11:3-7). It is difficult to understand – Solomon, the king who built the temple, also constructed an altar of child sacrifice. Perhaps he thought to himself, "These gods are just in addition to Jehovah." But to worship God this way is to not worship Him at all. Because he abandoned God, there was collateral damage that followed.

After Solomon's death, the once-united nation of Israel split into two kingdoms. Jeroboam ruled the Northern Kingdom of Israel, while Rehoboam, Solomon's son, reigned over the Southern Kingdom of Judah. The temple of the Lord, the only authorized place of sacrifice, was located in Jerusalem in Judah. According to the Law, the people were required to travel there for worship and sacrifices. Fearing that these pilgrimages would turn the hearts of his people back to Rehoboam, Jeroboam saw their loyalty to the temple as a threat to his own power.

Rather than trusting in God, Jeroboam devised a more subtle strategy – control through convenience. It was as if Jeroboam said to himself, "Why threaten them to keep them from leaving when I can seduce them with comfort instead?" Jeroboam planned to lead the people into a dangerous compromise that mirrored the rebellion at Sinai. He crafted two golden calves and said to the people, "It is too much for you to go up to Jerusalem. Here are your gods, Israel, who brought you up out of Egypt" (1 Kings 12:28, KJV). By planting one in Dan (the most northern part of the kingdom) and one in Bethel (only a few miles from Jerusalem) he was saying, "You don't have to go that far to worship!" Convenient Christianity, which is comfortable and not costly, is a counterfeit. Convenient

Christianity can be as far from God as possible, while at the same time, position itself close to the real thing.

C.S. Lewis said, "If you want a religion to make you feel comfortable, I certainly don't recommend Christianity."[24] We are not called to consent to a comfortable life unchallenged by conviction. Our walk with God comes at a cost, which is reasonable and rewarding. Like the golden calf in Bethel, trying to live for God through comfort and convenience is so close, yet so far from genuine relationship. There are many compromising positions we can place ourselves in that may look close in proximity to where we should be, but they are cheap imitations. For Israel, stopping at Bethel was the path of compromise. For us, it could look like pulling away from faithfulness to the body of Christ. Perhaps we are faithful in church attendance, yet we refuse to grow in holiness. In many ways, Israel's new gods looked just like their old ones. Idolatry attempts to rewrite your history of deliverance. Convenience and comfort didn't get you out of Egypt – what delivered you out of bondage was the decision to allow conviction to make you uncomfortable; what got you out was the decision to repent and allow the grace of God to pull you out; what delivered you and secures your future is your dependence on Jesus Christ alone.

If you feel like Solomon today – someone who began the journey well but made destructive choices that fractured your legacy – there is hope. Maybe your story feels like it started in ruins, and you wonder if your legacy is beyond repair. For you too, there is hope. The Lord's promise of restoration to Israel is something we can cling to as well when we turn to Him:

> There, in a foreign land, you will worship idols made from wood and stone—gods that neither see nor hear nor eat nor smell. But from there you will search again for the Lord your God. And if you search for him with all your heart and soul, you will find him. "In the distant future, when you are suffering all these things, you will finally return to the Lord your God and listen to what he tells you. For the Lord your God is a merciful God; he will not abandon you or destroy you or forget the solemn covenant he made with your ancestors. (Deuteronomy 4:28-31, NLT)

We close this book by returning to the beginning. When God commanded Abraham to sacrifice Isaac, child sacrifice was not an unfamiliar concept in the ancient world. But by staying Abraham's hand and providing a substitute offering, God was declaring something profound: He is not like the gods of this world. He is the God of life – the One who preserves your legacy, not one who demands its destruction. He gave His life so that you might live. He endured suffering so that you could inherit the hope of glory. "For the promise is unto you, and to your children, and to all that are afar off, even as many as the Lord our God shall call" (Acts 2:39, KJV).

Study Questions

1. In what ways are you affected by the legacy handed down to you? If you grew up in dysfunction, have you been able to avoid harmful behaviors?

2. What is your legacy? In what ways can you put your future in the hands of God now?

3. Having a relationship with God while living with idolatry is impossible because idolatry demands that we focus on ourselves. We can take that into the context of marriage and family life. Idolatry destroys healthy relationships. If we worship idols, sacrifice is shoved into a corner somewhere and only pulled out when it's conveniently self-serving. Can you identify areas where your sacrifices are self-serving rather than flowing from your relationship with Jesus?

Endnotes

1 Bolding, J. (2023, December 31). Idolatry still a modern-day problem, Billy Graham says. *DeseretNews.* https://www.deseret.com/2012/4/27/20501682/idolatry-still-a-modern-day-problem-billy-graham-says/

2 *Characteristics of Christ's discples.* (n.d.). The Spurgeon Center. https://www.spurgeon.org/resource-library/sermons/characteristics-of-christs-disciples/#flipbook/

3 *Industrial revolution and technology.* (n.d.). https://education.nationalgeographic.org/resource/industrial-revolution-and-technology/

4 *Manifest Destiny on rails: The Transcontinental Railroad.* (n.d.). Midwest Model Railroad. https://midwestmodelrr.com/blog/manifest-destiny-on-rails-the-transcontinental-railroad/

5 Warren W. Wiersbe, *The Bible Exposition Commentary, Volume II Ephesians-Revelation* (Colorado, Springs: David C. Cook, 1989), 342.

6 Unknown, U. (n.d.). *Cross My Heart, Part 5.* http://www.raymondwood-ward.com/uploads/1/4/0/4/14045200/cross_20my_20heart_20part_205.pdf

7 C.S. Lewis Institute. (2024, January 16). *The Transformation of our heart's desires - C.S. Lewis Institute.*

https://www.cslewisinstitute.org/resources/
the-transformation-of-our-hearts-desires/

8   *We become what we worship: a biblical theology
of idolatry.* (n.d.). Everand. https://www.everand.com/
read/523175934/We-Become-What-We-Worship-A-
Biblical-Theology-Of-Idolatry

9   GotQuestions.org. (2022, January 4).
GotQuestions.org. https://www.gotquestions.org/
golden-calf.html

10   Enduring Word. (2024, March 20). *Enduring
Word Bible Commentary Romans Chapter 1.* https://endur-
ingword.com/bible-commentary/romans-1/

11   A quote from *Not a Fan.* (n.d.). https://www.
goodreads.com/quotes/921717-what-you-win-them-
with-is-what-you-win-them

12   *Praise the Lord (vv. 6-8). - Warren Wiersbe BE
Bible Study Series - Bible Gateway.* (n.d.). https://www.
biblegateway.com/resources/wiersbe-be-bible-study/
praise-lord-vv-6-8

13   John Bevere. (2023a, June 11). *Looking For
Intimacy with God? | Lesson 2 of Drawing Near | Study
with John Bevere* [Video]. YouTube. https://www.you-
tube.com/watch?v=DcbjnR_ZFVg

14   *Please don't say you need me: Biblical
Answers for Codependency.* (n.d.). Everand.
https://www.everand.com/read/170442243/

Please-Don-t-Say-You-Need-Me-Biblical-Answers-for-Codependency

15   Linney, S. (2024, January 5). *What is HALT? The dangers of being hungry, angry, lonely or tired* | American Addiction Centers. American Addiction Centers. https://americanaddictioncenters.org/blog/common-stressors-recovery

16   Capital Community Church. (2015, July 9). *"The Other Side of Prayer" - Stan Gleason* [Video]. YouTube. https://www.youtube.com/watch?v=3N_JbyLtnwI

17   A quote from *Paths to Power.* (n.d.). https://www.goodreads.com/quotes/10834118-the-hardest-deception-to-cure-is-that-which-is-self-imposed

18   Guzik, D. (n.d.). *Study Guide for Isaiah 44. Blue Letter Bible.* https://www.blueletterbible.org/comm/guzik_david/study-guide/isaiah/isaiah-44.cfm

19   Enduring Word. (2025, February 11). *Enduring Word Bible Commentary Mark Chapter 8.* https://enduringword.com/bible-commentary/mark-8/

20   Silvious, J. (n.d.). *Please don't say you need me.* Zondervan Publishing House.

21   *Exodus 20 Berean Study Bible.* (n.d.). https://biblehub.com/study/exodus/20.htm

22   Please don't say you need me: Biblical Answers for Codependency. (n.d.-b). Everand. https://www.everand.com/read/170442243/

Please-Don-t-Say-You-Need-Me-Biblical-Answers-for-Codependency

23 Wiersbe, W. W. (2007). *The Wiersbe Bible Commentary.* David C. Cook. https://storage.snappages. site/7STCWP/assets/files/The-Wiersbe-Bible-Commentary-Old-Testame-90.pdf

24 *Quotes by C.S. Lewis.* (n.d.). Grace Quotes. https://gracequotes.org/author-quote/c-s-lewis/page/2/